LEARNING FOR LIFE

The foundations for lifelong learning

David H. Hargreaves

First published in Great Britain in June 2004 by

The Policy Press
University of Bristol
Fourth Floor
Beacon House
Queen's Road
Bristol BS8 1QU
UK

Tel +44 (0)117 331 4054
Fax +44 (0)117 331 4093
e-mail tpp-info@bristol.ac.uk
www.policypress.org.uk

British Library Cataloguing in Publication Data
A catalogue record for this book is available from the British Library

Library of Congress Cataloging-in-Publication Data
A catalog record for this book has been requested

ISBN 1 86134 597 6 paperback

David H. Hargreaves is a Fellow of Wolfson College, Cambridge.

Cover design by Qube Design Associates, Bristol
Front cover: photograph supplied by kind permission of the Science Photo Library
Printed and bound in Great Britain by Hobbs the Printers Ltd, Southampton

Contents

Foreword by Christopher Brookes, The Lifelong Learning Foundation   v

Acknowledgements   viii

one   Introduction   1

two   Curriculum   5

three   Assessment   15

four   Pedagogy   25

five   Advice and guidance   35

six   Information, communication and learning technologies   45

seven   School design   55

eight   Innovation   65

nine   The teaching profession   75

ten   Leadership   81

eleven   Firm foundations   91

Sources and suggestions   101

Appendix: Participants in the seminar   105

Index   107

Foreword

As well as securing our economic future, learning has a wider contribution.
It helps make ours a civilised society, develops the spiritual side of our lives
and promotes active citizenship. Learning enables people to play a full part
in their community. It strengthens the family, the neighbourhood and
consequently the nation. It helps us fulfil our potential and opens doors to
a love of music, art and literature. That is why we value learning for its own
sake as well as for the equality of opportunity it brings.... To realise our
ambition, we must all develop and sustain a regard for learning at whatever
age.

It is now over six years since the publication by the then Department for
Education and Employment of the consultative document, *The learning age: A
renaissance for a new Britain*. David Blunkett's Foreword to this document was
memorable not only for the quality of its prose; in addition, it outlined in a
lyrical, enlightened vision the seminal features of a culture of learning suited to
21st-century Britain. Writing in 2004, it is difficult to find compelling evidence
that there has been in England a significant and sustained move toward the
creation of a coherent, engaging, accessible culture of lifelong learning.

Whither is fled the visionary gleam?
Where is it now, the glory and the dream?

Wordsworth's famous lines lament the loss of intimations of immortality in
early childhood, but it does not require an unreasonable exercise of artistic
licence to suggest that, for many, they express with equal sadness the fading of
those intimations of lifelong learning articulated by David Blunkett.

Why has the 'dream' proved so difficult to transform into reality? Over the
past five years I have been offered many answers to this question, ranging in
content and style from the relatively restrained observation that:

Looking back at *The learning age*, it is now clear that there was a significant
cognitive and emotional dissonance between the mood and content of the
Foreword and the substance of what followed

through expressions of concern about the number of 'initiatives' being
introduced into schools and classrooms, to the more forthright, although not
always substantiated, critique of Whitehall's perhaps outdated approach to the
challenge of developing a coherent lifelong learning strategy. While there is no
doubting the extent to which views such as these express deeply-felt concerns
about the future of education in England, it is less clear that they offer a balanced

and feasible way forward, taking into account both short-term opportunities and longer-term imperatives.

The timing and pace of change are critical, but often neglected, issues in creating a culture of lifelong learning. A former British Prime Minister once noted that "A week is a long time in politics"; where the requirement is to introduce fundamental changes into a system as complex and deeply embedded as compulsory education in England, it is at least arguable that six years is a relatively short period. The 'time' factor in this context is difficult to weigh, but it is an important consideration to be borne in mind when assessing the effectiveness of the measures taken since 1998, and of those that should and can be brought forward during the next few years.

For the Lifelong Learning Foundation, whose very existence is predicted on a belief in the value and feasibility of learning for and through life, the pervasive lack of clarity about the meaning of one of the key terms in use – *lifelong learning* – is an obvious source of concern. Today, a taxonomy of interpretations would range from a conventional, minimalist 'makeover' of all forms of post-16, formal education (with the predictable exception of higher education) to the transformatory ideal of an interconnected process of cumulative learning, extending from 'cradle-to-grave' and having the learner at the heart of the process – the Lifelong Learning Foundation's position.

It was against this background that early in 2002 we asked David Hargreaves to lead a project aimed at:

- creating an overarching intellectual framework to enable us to develop a deeper understanding of lifelong learning; and
- identifying those key changes – in policy and practice – that would need to be brought forward for this understanding to be realised;
- offering an informed, constructive perspective on the process of change itself.

The outcome was a series of 11 seminars, held between May 2002 and October 2003, focused on the theme, *Shaping policies for lifelong learning: a radical approach*. Six leading-edge thinkers and practitioners, drawn from across the spectrum of formal education, were invited to each event; each group explored a separate, but related, dimension of the challenge. As well as leading the series, David guided the process of enquiry that unfolded. This book is the outcome of that series.

In supporting the project the Foundation has been particularly mindful of two considerations:

- Whatever radical sentiment may be entertained, there is at the moment, as far as compulsory education is concerned, only 'one show in town', and it is consuming a fair chunk of taxpayers' money. There is therefore a strong case for making improvements to the immediate and short-term effectiveness of the existing education system one of the critical themes throughout the series. Throughout his analysis, David Hargreaves draws our attention to the many opportunities for making improvements of this type that already exist, or that will arise within the next year or so, for example, in arrangements for the '14-19' age group following the work of the Tomlinson Group.

• In the medium to longer term, there may be good prima facie reasons for supposing that something rather more than incremental change will need to be countenanced if the current education system in England is to retain its credibility as the preferred 'supply-side' response to individuals' demand for learning. Take, for example, the issues of 'motivation' and 'behaviour'. Fifty years ago, perhaps even 25 years ago, it may have been reasonable for governments to assume that they had a fairly accurate understanding of why young people regarded going to school as worthwhile and inherently 'good' and why their behaviour within school, by and large, reflected this consensus. Today, there are reasons – intellectual and practical – to doubt whether such a consensus exists – or, if it does, to question the perceptions, attitudes and values on which it is based. One has only to ask about the impact of media and consumerism on young people, about the force of peer groups and about the growing and beguiling accessibility of online information and learning to get a sense of why and how much the 'old order' might be changing.

In commending this book to all stakeholders in the education, business and policy communities, we believe it offers an intellectually powerful, relevant and accessible perspective on the changes that are needed if the education system of the 21st century and beyond is to equip and motivate individuals to meet the demands and challenges that will face them in managing their lives and their work. For most of recorded history, it could have been said of *Homo sapiens* that being alive was the essential precondition for living; today and for the foreseeable future, however, to live we need the capacity, the opportunity and the sustained will to learn.

Christopher Brookes
The Lifelong Learning Foundation

Acknowledgements

The Lifelong Learning Foundation wishes to record its profound gratitude to the participants in the seminar series which led to the writing of this book, and in particular to David H. Hargreaves for both leading the series and preparing this text.

ONE

Introduction

"The concept of lifelong learning has been allowed to become tired and the big picture fractures into its many component parts." (Goodison Group Seminar)

"Until quite recently most education occurred incidentally. Unlike incidental learning which is natural and inevitable, formal schooling is deliberate intervention and must justify itself." (Paul Goodman)

Lifelong learning is often held to begin when compulsory education ends, when students are 16, and sometimes at the end of later full-time education, such as graduation at a university. This applies to the Department for Education and Skills, where lifelong learning seems to have little, if anything, to do with school education. Lifelong learning should mean what the term plainly says: learning lasts for life – 'cradle to grave' – and so begins when we are born and embark on the adventure we are well programmed to pursue: *learning*. The principal function of formal education, therefore, should be to help people to learn, embracing both *content* (knowledge, skill and understanding of various kinds) and *process* (the motivation and ability to learn successfully).

This book assumes that whether people are motivated to learn beyond the end of compulsory education, and have the capacity to do so, depends very much on what happens to them during school years. The foundations of lifelong learning are laid during these years. In the 21st century, getting these learner-centred foundations right is of immense importance for the well-being of individuals, for thriving communities and for the prosperity of the nation. Education of young people helps to prepare them both for life and also for remaking the world in which that life is lived.

In the following chapters we explore what happens in school years that weakens rather than strengthens these foundations, what might be done to put things right, and what implications this might have for policies for school education. This entails being open-minded about how education during school years might develop over coming decades, how the content and processes involved might have to change, and how the outcomes we expect of such education might be different in kind and evaluated in different ways.

This book does not start with a new vision, a detailed picture of lifelong learning and how that would make for a different education service in a different society. The education service, like society itself, is the product of many forces, evolving and changing of its own accord as these forces develop and interact in complex ways. So it seems sensible to start from the government's own vision, which raises expectations of school education as British society and its economy becomes more knowledge-based, combined with a pressing need for greater social cohesion – all of which implies a commitment to lifelong learning for all. To this I add some explicit commitments, as sketched above; ones that I believe are widely shared and are relatively uncontroversial. Since the path to the future inevitably begins from where we are now, the titles of the chapters that follow are conventional and familiar precisely because they reflect the status quo in terms of policy, whether well established or emergent. At the end of the book it will be easier to offer a vision of a society and education service characterised by lifelong learning because the route from here to there – sometimes easy, sometime difficult – will have been explored.

Running through the book are five themes, which for most people will not be familiar or obvious educational topics and which might have been chapters of their own. The first and most important theme is *learning how to learn*, which, in a kind of paradox, makes part of the content of learning not a subject, such as mathematics or geography, but learning itself. If, during our school years, we could not merely learn a specific content but could also learn how the process of learning itself works and can be improved, then we would be better equipped for all later learning.

The second is *generic skills*, or skills that are not specific to a particular content or context but are transferable and applicable to many different types of content and context. The skill of 'problem solving' is generic, whereas the skill of solving problems in algebra is more specific. If generic skills can be acquired during school years, then all our learning would be enhanced.

The third is the *project*, which refers to a way of organising learning and teaching in a way that differs from the ubiquitous concept of the lesson we all immediately associate with life at school. Lessons are the hallowed form of provision in educational institutions, but the learning in which we engage during life does not come neatly bundled up as a lesson. In life we learn in trying to accomplish larger and more complex tasks in real situations where success or failure have very real consequences. Such projects are more characteristic of our lives outside and beyond the school – in the home, at work and during leisure or community activities. If we could learn to manage projects while at school, we would be better equipped for life's multifarious projects.

The fourth is *mentors*, the people who assist and support learning, and a term that is far less familiar to the world of school than the word 'teacher'. We do not have contact with formal, professional teachers throughout our lives, but lifelong learning depends on the availability of mentors or coaches to help us to learn – and our own capacity for mentoring contributes to the lifelong learning of others.

The fifth (and least felicitous) is *personalisation*, or the process of ensuring that educational provision meets the needs and aspirations of every individual learner. Much formal education, especially during school years, is producer-led; could schools become, like much adult education, more sensitive to their clients?

These five concepts – learning how to learn, generic skills, the project, mentors and personalisation – are the foundational themes that serve as threads through the following chapters. They are introduced and explained as we go along, and are brought together in the final chapter, which will show how in combination they become central concepts in a vision of an education service that can justifiably be said to support lifelong learning.

TWO

Curriculum

Curricular changes of real significance almost always involve changes in method and ways of working. (Lawrence Stenhouse)

It is conventional to speak of mere knowledge ... as of itself imparting a peculiar dignity to its possessor. I do not share this reverence for knowledge as such. It all depends on who has the knowledge and what he does with it. That knowledge which adds greatness to character is knowledge so handled as to transform every phase of immediate experience. (A.N. Whitehead)

The curriculum, especially when schooling is under discussion, is usually defined as the content of what is taught by teachers and (supposedly) learned by students. As long as there have been schools there has been some kind of official or formal curriculum; and the debates about what it should contain, in what terms it should be expressed, and who should determine it, have been many and varied. When a society comes to accept the need for lifelong learning, does this make any difference to how we should talk about and determine the curriculum and shape policy decisions at national or local levels, in the school or in the classroom?

Such questions quickly touch on the fundamental purposes of education, in terms of both how they have come to shape the present and how they might need to change in a society in which lifelong learning is fostered. Four factors that drive discussion and debate about the curriculum may be identified (Figure 1).

Figure 1: Factors driving the curriculum

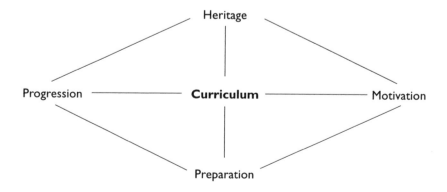

All societies have to some degree used the school curriculum as a system of cultural transmission to the young. Culture is used in two senses. First, it concerns the fundamental values of a society and its social institutions. Currently the emphasis here is on citizenship education, following several decades of diffuse development of personal, social and health education, in addition to religious education. Second, it concerns 'high culture', or in Matthew Arnold's famous words, "acquainting ourselves with the best that has been known and said, and thus with the history of the human spirit". Taken together, these constitute the *heritage* aspect of the curriculum with its purpose of socialising the young into society, into its values, traditions, culture and achievements.

Much socialisation is common to all members of society as we learn the fundamental values of democratic society and respect for the rights and dignity of other people. But the school curriculum has had an additional function, that of preparing young people for their particular place in society after they leave school. In the past the purpose was to select them for their position in the social class system, to allocate them to an occupation, and, in the case of a minority, to qualify them for the later stages of education, especially university. This social reproduction has become less salient as schooling, like society itself, has become more 'open', with a greater emphasis on the choices – of school and (after 14) of subjects – that students (and their parents) make for themselves rather than what education does to them. The curriculum remains class-related, at least explicitly in school, but now less so than in the past. As a correspondent to a newspaper put it:

> In the days before the 11-plus, I was a 'scholarship boy' who won one of the relatively few places available to children of the poor at the local grammar school. We were greeted by the headmaster with the words: 'Of course there is no question of people like you going to university – we will not therefore waste time teaching you Latin, Greek, German or French. A socialist society will doubtless have a great need of clerks and that is what you will be educated to be.'

As the minimum age for leaving school lengthened from 12 to 16 during the 20th century, *preparation* has become more fluid, as the educational, social and occupational destinations of students are less predictable and ascribed. Moreover, the choices that school students make are not as irreversible as they once were: our models of the education system are less like ladders and more like climbing frames. Once it is accepted that most people will need to engage in various forms of education and training throughout their lives, then preparation becomes more important and less specific. Dispositions and attitudes are often said to be more important than knowledge, which is now claimed by some to become quickly out of date, and the most important skills are taken to be transferable ones. There is some exaggeration here: much of the knowledge that is acquired in school, especially but not exclusively during the primary years, is the indispensable background knowledge of what it means to be an educated person, and its value does not diminish with age. Even when such knowledge is modified or replaced, the recognition that knowledge can sometimes change is itself educative. To assign more importance to skill acquisition may mean that we have to be more selective in what established knowledge is transmitted through schooling; and this is merely a reiteration of an old problem that the school curriculum is inherently a selection of knowledge, and as such will always be a contentious matter. As the Scots used to put it, the curriculum is like a shelf of books: there is always pressure to add new volumes, but a reluctance to weed out some well-established works to make space to accommodate them. As we shall see, there is a way round this.

Student *motivation* was in the past far less important than it is today. Whether and what young people wanted to learn willingly was not a relevant consideration: those with low motivation left school as soon as they could or dropped out of education when it no longer commanded their interest. As the school leaving age was raised, and as jobs for early leavers declined, means had to be found of attracting them to remain in, and be committed to, formal education. It is the curriculum that has been seen to be at the heart of the motivational crisis: the danger is that it might be 'boring' and the challenge is to make it 'relevant'. When the school leaving age was raised from 15 to 16 in 1974, many teachers were anxious to find a means of motivating the first cohort of students to be unwillingly trapped in school for the extra year. One desperate teacher in a secondary modern school for girls constructed the whole of the curriculum for the bottom set during this final year around the theme of 'My wedding day'. This fusion of motivation and preparation would today command less respect than it did a quarter of a century ago, in part because we blame student disaffection on poor teaching as much as on inappropriate content. Indeed, we do not know the degree to which student disengagement is attributable to inappropriate curriculum content or to inappropriate teaching – or even a combination of the two.

For this reason, *heritage* and *motivation* are often seen to be in conflict. Many young people experience some of our cultural heritage as extremely tedious, at least as it is transmitted through the school curriculum. The recurring debate about the place of Shakespeare in the curriculum is a case in point. Those who want to reduce the amount of Shakespeare in favour of other kinds of literature that students might find more interesting are denounced in parts of the press as unpatriotic philistines; and education ministers take fright less they be accused yet again of 'dumbing down' the curriculum. We reach a kind of stalemate in which the unsatisfactory parts of the National Curriculum and the GCSE in English and English Literature escape a desirable revision. (There is, of course, an obvious solution. Students sometimes find Shakespeare dull because they read the plays in classrooms rather than seeing them performed in theatres. If we made it a requirement that any Shakespeare play studied in school had also to be seen in the theatre, then much student disenchantment would evaporate. If this requirement entailed increasing the number of theatre companies performing Shakespeare regularly, this would enrich our national heritage to every one's benefit.)

The tension between heritage and motivation is expressed in changing conceptions of *an entitlement curriculum*. The origins of this concept lie in the writings of HM Inspectorate in the 1980s. Their surveys had shown that the transition from the tripartite to comprehensive system had disturbed curriculum structures. It was assumed in many comprehensive schools that the grammar school curriculum was to become the curriculum for all students in place of the less academic and more varied curriculum of many secondary modern schools. In practice, this did not work very well, so 'options' after the third year of secondary school were provided to capture the declining motivation of 'less academic' students. The options provided students with real choices, and some of these choices were soon regarded as undesirable. Many girls, for instance, opted out of science completely or at least out of the physical sciences. When inspectors found very wide variations in what was being offered in Years 10 and 11 (that is, 14- to 16-year-olds in what became key stage four), they argued that all young people were entitled to a common curriculum during their secondary schooling. This approach was crucial in determining the nature and content of the National Curriculum of 1988. Being *entitled* to a curriculum meant that it was *compulsory* for students, whether they were motivated by it or not.

Before the age of 14, that is, during the first three key stages, the National Curriculum rules: students have little choice over a compulsory curriculum. Of course, everyone acknowledges that the basics – literacy and numeracy – have to be acquired by every child, for without them they are denied access to the rest of the curriculum. Even here, however, care has to be taken. There is evidence that the literacy strategy in primary schools is increasing children's *skill* in reading, but this seems to be achieved alongside, and possibly at the cost of, a declining *interest* in reading. In what sense is it a good education if one acquires a skill but takes little pleasure in exercising it? But the strong case for insisting on early literacy and numeracy is more difficult to sustain when applied to parts of our cultural heritage provided after the age of 14. Literature is a case in point. People report that in later life they discover Shakespeare or Jane Austen *in spite of* how these authors were taught at school rather than *because of* their formal education. It is hard to acquire the basics later in life if they are neglected during school years, and failure here incurs a heavy personal and social cost in adult life. But the same cannot be said of aspects of our cultural heritage, where there are many opportunities in adult life for discovering them through mature learning: jamming them into a compulsory curriculum for all at certain ages may damage the very motivation and enjoyment the compulsion is intended to achieve.

Over time, lack of motivation for some subjects forced modifications: some subjects of the National Curriculum could be 'dis-applied', and these arrangements were widely adopted for a minority of students and particularly in modern foreign languages. The tension between entitlement and choice continues to this day. In the government's reform of the 14-19 phase, the key stage four curriculum is to be reduced to a core of English, Mathematics, Science and IT. 'Disapplication' is abolished and other subjects, including a modern foreign language, become optional. 'Entitlement as compulsion' is replaced by 'entitlement to access', that is, the school is obliged to provide the subject but the student is not obliged to accept what is provided. Objectors to the change in status of modern foreign languages use utilitarian argument ('we are members of a multilingual Europe') rather than an appeal to heritage to defend the *status quo*. At its heart, however, the change is that, outside a small number of core subjects, students over the age of 14 are now *entitled not to be bored* by their study of the school curriculum. If a choice has to be made between the motivation of adolescent students and their educational entitlement, it is motivation that wins.

As young people have received, with various degrees of enthusiasm, a much longer period of education, then *progression* in learning has also become more important. It is not enough simply to learn: one has to experience continuity in what is provided in the curriculum from stage to stage and year to year and to make progress over time, so that knowledge, skill and understanding develop and grow. The National Curriculum was introduced in part to provide for better continuity and progression, but the school curriculum is still experienced by many students as a disjointed series of topics and tasks that lack internal coherence within a subject and with few explicit links between subjects. For those on what is becoming the mainstream pathway through A-level to higher education, continuity and progression are relatively easy to perceive. But for those on other pathways, especially the vocational, continuity and progression are easily lost in the various transitions between courses and institutions. Not surprisingly, it is these students who drop out of formal education most quickly and in the largest numbers. It is precisely these students who are most at risk of becoming the disadvantaged who disappear from lifelong learning.

Taken together, the now pressing demands of student motivation and progression bear heavily on the profession as teachers are forced to re-conceptualise the relationship between teaching and learning. For in the past, the teacher was the crucial gateway to knowledge, one to which learners had few alternatives. The teacher's job was to teach, as he or she thought best, and if necessary *make* the students learn. If they showed signs of rebellion, then the teacher cajoled them into compliance, making them sufficiently tractable so that they suffered their education for as long as they remained in school. In the age of lifelong learning, the teacher has to motivate students to learn the curriculum at hand, as always. Ensuring student tractability among disengaged students will no longer do. Now the teacher must ensure that students are motivated to continue to learn beyond the current stage, and, most demanding of all, must provide them with the skills and tools that will enable them to be successful in that further learning. For more learning than ever will take place outside of institutions dedicated to learning and without a teacher. It was ever thus, of course: but the fact is now being widely recognised. Such informal learning is at the heart of lifelong learning and because this learning takes forms that differ strongly from those in schools, there will be important lessons for educators to learn here.

Today, then, learning is the priority and the task of teaching is to ensure that learning, and the motivation and capacity to learn, are secured in the student, now and indefinitely into the future, in formal educational institutions under the guidance of teachers and in the outside world without being formally taught. If the goal is lifelong learning, then the nature of the entitlement might also change. Entitlement to heritage or freedom from boredom could be replaced by a lifelong learning entitlement:

- to be helped to love learning;
- to be taught how to learn well;
- to be provided with appropriate opportunities to learn;

although these entitlements could be honoured only if the learner accepted the obligation to become a lifelong learner in the first place. And that still leaves open the question of the content of the curriculum.

This new vision of the changing purposes of education for lifelong learning, while receiving much rhetorical support from education ministers and from the teaching profession, is testing to the limit how we talk about the curriculum. Indeed, the basic concepts that have hitherto been used to discuss and debate *curriculum* itself, rather than its associated purposes, are proving to be inadequate to the task.

The curriculum is constructed out of a set of 'bricks', and deciding the nature of these bricks is now a contentious matter. Conventionally the bricks are a set of subjects that are academic *disciplines*, such as Mathematics, or *fields of study* that comprise more than one discipline, such as Geography. These have sometimes been regarded as quite arbitrary collections of an arbitrary selection of knowledge, but others have argued that they are fundamentally different ways of knowing, with their own concepts, modes of enquiry and means of distinguishing the good from the bad. Some famous examples, in chronological order, are:

- 'forms of knowledge', such as logic and mathematics, physical sciences, aesthetic, ethics and so on, as suggested by the philosopher Paul Hirst; or
- 'areas of experience', such as mathematical, scientific, linguistic, aesthetic and creative, spiritual and so on, as suggested by HM Inspectorate; or
- 'multiple intelligences', such as logical–mathematical, musical, spatial, interpersonal and so on, as suggested by Howard Gardner;

but none of these has displaced the concept 'subjects' in the working vocabulary of most teachers or the organisation of the school day in most places.

Most secondary teachers studied a subject at university and think of themselves as teachers of that discipline ('a maths teacher,' for example). The school day is divided into (usually relatively short) blocks of time, each of which is dedicated to one of these subjects taught by the appropriate specialist teacher: this makes up the timetable of the school curriculum. Attempts are regularly made to combine different subjects (for example, 'integrated humanities') so that students might experience at first hand the linkages between disciplines, especially when they are applied to real-world problems. However, these are difficult to teach and it is often said that students fail to master the nature of the individual disciplines. Many have complained that the National Curriculum is largely expressed in terms of these subjects/disciplines and has stifled innovation in this regard, but many secondary teachers would have been deeply confused had it been constructed out of rather different 'bricks'.

The National Curriculum is not, however, built quite crudely out of the *knowledge* contained in each subject, but rather specifies in addition *understanding* and *skill*, which for teachers and students are aspects of the curriculum that are far more difficult to handle. Given that the dominant view of the curriculum is that it contains *bodies of knowledge*, it is not surprising that the concept of *skills* – or similar terms such as competence – has tended to capture the imagination of those who seek to re-conceptualise the curriculum. Skills have an established place in the mainstream secondary curriculum, notably in the form of the key skills qualifications for literacy, numeracy and IT, but their relationship to subjects, not least to English and Mathematics, is obscure.

The most impressive, influential and thorough reworking of the curriculum in terms of skills has been the Royal Society of Arts 'Opening Minds' project (Bayliss, 1999), which seeks to make the curriculum competence-led rather than information-led. This neatly capitalises on the current fashion to judge educational achievement in terms of student outcomes rather than teacher inputs, and on a strong future orientation with a concern about how young people will be able to manage their lives and work in a rapidly changing society. Thus the central concepts for the curriculum assume the form of a set of competences:

- for learning
- for citizenship
- for relating to people
- for managing situations
- for managing information.

When skills are emphasised at the expense of knowledge, conservative educationists leap to the defence of heritage. It is not easy to recast the National Curriculum, or even more, the main qualifications such as the GCSE and A-level, in terms of these very different 'bricks'. So conservatives claim that this change of emphasis is tantamount to a 'dumbing down' of a true education that is justified for its own sake with a curriculum firmly grounded in knowledge deriving from our heritage. They bewail its replacement by what they see as a mixture of instrumental vocationalism and a mishmash of skills that purportedly promote the 'lifelong learning' that is said to be essential in a 'knowledge economy'. Such antitheses are constantly advanced but rarely contribute to progress in discussion. As Mary Warnock (1977) has rightly observed, there are many things that are *both* inherently good *and* good as an instrument or a means of doing something else. Health, food and love meet both criteria, so if education joins them it is in good company. This unproductive battle between the self-assured conservatives and the more tentative radicals is preventing the creation of the new curriculum language in which to harness the best of the past and the need for change in education to meet the demands of a very different future.

More radical possibilities are being aired, such as the Association for Science Education's conception of a curriculum made up of 'big ideas' + 'key processes' + 'key stories' and Howard Gardner's (1999a, 1999b) personal preference for a curriculum organised around three topics: the theory of evolution, the music of Mozart and the Holocaust. But these are at the edge of our current thinking, which is characterised by scepticism about the old curriculum framework, especially the National Curriculum, but nervousness towards radical change. The inclination in this mood of disquiet is to feel drawn to concepts of skills and competences as providing the most promising direction of travel, even if it is towards a hazy destination. Thus we have a range of *generic skills*, often called 'soft' or 'wider' skills or competences, that are held to be important for lifelong learning and life in a knowledge economy, where what students have learned in school can be applied in the range of contexts they encounter in later life. These usually include:

- managing one's own learning
- problem solving
- thinking
- research, enquiry and investigation
- invention, enterprise and entrepreneurship
- communication
- social and interpersonal
- teamwork
- leadership.

Learning how to learn is sometimes seen as one of these generic skills and sometimes as something distinctive and more fundamental.

How generic skills are to be integrated with the ordinary school curriculum is far from obvious – for they are rarely held to be a complete alternative to what is now taught in school. There is a lack of clarity about this practical task of finding a way in which to bind these new curriculum 'bricks' to the older language of subjects and disciplines. The nature of *progression* in these generic skills – what precisely it means to get better or achieve greater mastery in them – also remains to be clarified. These essential tasks, I believe, can be achieved only through some deep curriculum innovation. However, part of the price we paid for the National Curriculum is that 'curriculum development' became something of an oxymoron. Some argue that curriculum innovation will be stifled until the National Curriculum is abolished. But I have yet to see an alternative that retains the critical advantages that were advanced to justify it in 1988 – such as, making it easier for mobile students to avoid having to master a completely new curriculum when moving to a new school, or the reduction in 'topics' that were repeated in different years in primary schools or after the transition to secondary school. Giving every school a high degree of autonomy over the curriculum had many drawbacks: pre-1988 was not a golden age for the curriculum to which we ought unthinkingly to return.

Yet there are many evolutionary, if unspectacular, developments at the edge of the mainstream curriculum that are rich in revolutionary potential. One example is work-related learning, the only new addition to the compulsory part of the secondary curriculum as proposed by the government in its 14-19 reforms. Many of those who were consulted thought it a good idea of itself, and it might also contribute to the raising of the status of the vocational aspects of education, build on the success or work experience, and offer students more opportunity to undertake motivating work-related activity outside school. Nowadays it is not so much about preparation for specific areas of working life but rather learning that working life now involves the capacity for self-directed learning. In the industrial age learning to put up with a boring education was preparation for a boring job in the factory. Today *learning how to learn* in school is a preparation for learning how to learn at work. If done well, work-related learning will open the way to examining:

- how and why people learn in very different ways in work settings;
- why people are highly motivated to learn at work;
- why *mentoring* and coaching in various forms of apprenticeship are more satisfying to both sides than some conventional teacher and student roles;
- how the world outside school is rich in opportunities to learn if we knew how to exploit them better;
- how learning 'out there' is more risky, more vital, more innovative.

I believe that the new language for the curriculum will follow changes in educational practice, such as the growth of work-related learning, rather than precede and shape them. When new and more satisfactory ways of 'doing the curriculum' have been discovered, only then shall we invent the language in which to expound what we know and do. Until then the main issues are likely to turn around the problem of curriculum provision – who is to provide it and where? For the curriculum is bursting out of its conventional constraints, which are the school as an institution, with qualified teachers who teach it, all in classrooms organised around a timetable of subjects. For all these structures are designed for the convenience of the professional, full-time teachers, not because they are the best ways in which young people can learn. The revolution is nurtured by the shift in priority from teaching to learning, and many teachers do not yet see just how threatening this is likely to be for them. We are about to discover what *natural* learning is like – whether that is done through advances in the neuro-sciences or from observations of how people learn in everyday settings at home, at work, at play and in the community. Then we shall have to re-think the purposes of education and re-work the language of the curriculum. Indeed, a new language for the curriculum is a precondition of the innovation that will be required for lifelong learning, if the term is to mean more than continual opportunities for formal education. Such provision of greater access is an advance, but true lifelong learning requires that, through their initial educational experiences, learners come to want to learn throughout life – although whether they actually do so will also depend on the provision of the right opportunities to learn at every subsequent stage of life. The drivers of curriculum, such as heritage, preparation, progression and motivation, and the tensions between them, will endure, but the challenge of lifelong learning will have irreversibly changed the meaning of *curriculum*, and the curriculum will have changed the meaning of lifelong learning.

Is the same true for assessment?

THREE

Assessment

"I should have liked to be asked to say what I knew. They always tried to ask what I did not know. When I would willingly have displayed my knowledge, they sought to expose my ignorance. This sort of treatment had only one result: I did not do well in examinations." (Winston S. Churchill)

Formal testing has moved much too far in the direction of assessing knowledge of questionable importance in ways that show little transportability. The understanding that schools ought to inculcate is virtually invisible on such instruments; quite different forms of assessment need to be implemented if we are to document student understandings. (Howard Gardner, 1999a)

It is a matter of almost universal agreement in the education service – outside the Department for Education and Skills (DfES), that is – that our assessment systems are in urgent need of reform. Sadly, there is no consensus about which aspects need to be reformed or in what ways. The weaknesses of the assessment systems – the plural is in order: that there are several of them is part of the problem – are rarely scrutinised from the point of view of lifelong learning. To do so here offers a distinctive perspective on the analysis of a major preoccupation of practitioners and policy makers. What are the problems that beset our assessment systems? How did they arise and what are their effects? What might be done to remedy the problems? And, most important of all, do the ways in which the learning and achievement of students are assessed during their school years affect their attitudes to, and participation in, lifelong learning?

At present, the most *common* complaint is that there is simply too much (formal) assessment: too many tests and examinations and too much course work. For some students, every year between the ages of 10 and 20 or so will contain at least one formal examination. An associated allegation is that the examinations boards – the unitary awarding bodies, AQA, Edexel and OCR – are inefficient, making too many mistakes in the way they handle GCSEs, AS- and A-levels. But many claim that however efficient the exam boards, the extent of formal assessment should be reduced, since it brings too much stress to students and teachers and distorts the true purposes and practices of education. The effect is that many students come to dislike their formal education, which is treated as something to be endured and from which an escape is sought, for some while still at school and for others immediately after taking their degree.

The most *disputed* complaint concerns the standards involved in these major public examinations. For many years the number of students entering for these examinations has risen steadily, but so also has the proportion of candidates who pass as well those who obtain the highest grades. Standards, say some critics, must therefore be slipping: the questions must be getting easier and/or the marking becoming more lenient. Ministers, examinations boards and many teachers and students object: young people are working harder and teachers are teaching more effectively, as OfSTED evidence confirms, so pass rates should increase and everyone should be congratulated on this significant educational improvement. Both sides have a case at a common sense level but neither argument can be proved beyond doubt, and similar difficulties are now arising over whether some A-level subjects are easier than others and therefore more likely to be selected by students to get the requisite points for entry to university.

Beneath these complaints that dominate media coverage are other concerns, many of a professional kind, that far less frequently enter public debate. The plethora of examinations means, it is claimed, that both teachers and students have become fixated on those parts of the curriculum that are being assessed – the core subjects in the National Curriculum in the case of the key stage national tests and the examination syllabuses in the case of GCSE, AS- and A-level courses. Teachers and students tend to push to the margin those topics that are not on the syllabus or whole subjects that are not examined formally, or even exclude them altogether; and they spend more and more time preparing for the test/examination. When an education system is under test pressure, what is not measured by the test tends not to count, for both teachers and students. The curriculum as planned, usually with breadth and balance in mind, becomes distorted. This is to invert the proper order of things, since one should surely decide the curriculum and then test the learning that ensues rather than decide what can be tested and allow only content that meets this criterion to find a place in the curriculum.

One consequence is that teachers begin to teach to the test. This is arguably no bad thing. If the test is a good test and generally worthwhile, what is wrong with teaching to the test? After all, if one joins a driving school to learn how to drive, one does not raise objections that the instructor is teaching to the demands of the driving test. The difficulty here is that most educational tests and examinations are not particularly good tests. Technical objections can be levelled against most of the tests/examinations for their low reliability and validity, including their weak capacity to predict further performance at a higher level, either in school or university. Indeed, it is not very rational of universities to base their admission policies largely on A-level grades and very small differences in grade between applicants. They continue to do so because it gives the appearance that admissions policies have some kind of objective basis and thus allegations of bias against certain kinds of pupil can be rebutted. The consequence of this is that students become obsessed with achieving the grades demanded by their preferred university and there is evidence that students will re-sit many AS- and A-level units simply to nudge up the final overall grade. The next step is for universities to invent their own tests that can discriminate the students they favour but have an apparent objectivity that interviews ostensibly lack. This will in turn generate a new industry of tutoring and courses to pass the new tests.

There is the more fundamental concern that of the three qualities that the National Curriculum and examination syllabuses require in successful learning – what a student *knows, understands* and *is able to do* – it is mainly one of these, *knowledge*, that the tests and examinations measure. *Skills* and *understanding* are much more difficult to measure, especially in written tests, which tend to focus on the student's capacity to memorise pieces of knowledge, or 'facts'. A good example of this may be found in the testing of Science. Pupils in the key stage two tests have over recent years shown a greater improvement in Science than in Maths or English. This may in part reflect that the way Science is taught has improved, but it is also explained in part by the fact that the tests measure memorised scientific facts much more effectively than an understanding and application of scientific processes, and that primary school teachers are themselves more comfortable with scientific facts than processes.

It is, of course, a grievous mistake to suggest that knowledge is unimportant. Knowledge is vital and there are no significant skills and no real understanding that can be acquired in the total absence of factual knowledge. The argument is not that we should dispense with the knowledge and replace it with skills and understanding, but rather that knowledge has become too dominant and is displacing skills and understanding from their rightful position alongside knowledge. Much knowledge – but by no means all – that is not linked in some way to skills and understanding will tend to be forgotten over time, whereas skills and understanding become more important than ever in the age of lifelong learning, since they often underpin later learning, including the acquisition of new knowledge, some of which changes rapidly in the modern world.

It is often the *generic skills*, not the subject-specific ones, that are least likely to be measured in tests and examinations – skills of problem solving, thinking, communication, teamwork, social relationships, and so on. These competences that almost all of us, including employers and higher education, now regard as vital, are of relatively low salience in most tests and examinations. The obvious example here is the key skills qualifications. The 'core' key skills of communication, numeracy and IT are qualifications that include a formal test, but the 'wider' key skills of problem solving, teamwork and responsibility for one's own learning are not tested, and are thus of secondary importance in both teaching and learning. It is the generic skills of greatest relevance to lifelong learning that are marginal and become so directly through the way in which they are dealt with by the assessment regime.

The quality most vulnerable to damage here is the capacity to *learn how to learn*, along with motivation to expend the effort to engage in continual learning. The problem is not so much that the tests and examinations do not measure these, but rather that our assessment systems so often seem to induce failure, injure built-in learning capabilities and ravage motivation. The damage is done in several ways. Up to the age of 14, pupils' most important formal assessments are the national key stage tests. The various levels can be used to check current attainment and serve as a baseline to measure progress as judged by later tests. For parents, the levels have the advantage of being more standardised than the old-style marks and comments that teachers used to offer in end-of-term and end-of-year reports. Yet the levels can be used as a generalised label for pupils – what is sometimes called categoric assessment – that is taken as an indicator of pupil ability, reinforcing conventional, stable categories such as 'intelligent' and 'less able'. The pupils, of course, quickly pick up the meaning and significance, both intellectual and social, of these levels-as-labels.

Among older students, performance in the GCSE becomes a crucial indicator of one's ability and intellectual worth. Originally the GCSE examination was devised to cover the majority of students, by joining the former O-level and the CSE into a single award. The grades A* to C reflect the O-level pass and they have become the benchmark, and the target, for GCSE performance. The effect, although doubtless unintended, is that the grades D to G are now rarely seen to be a pass at all – by students, parents, employers, further education colleges and, increasingly and perhaps inevitably, by teachers. Indeed, many students suppress the evidence of a D to G grade: it is better to imply one did not take the examination than to reveal that one took the exam and 'failed'. It goes without saying that students who achieve the lower levels in the national tests are the ones most likely to 'fail' the GCSE and form that group who leave school at the earliest opportunity with few or no qualifications. And of course, some of them had given up trying many years before, for not trying is not only a rational way of coping with failure but also a useful rationalisation of failure to protect a vulnerable self-esteem.

It is these young people whose disadvantages will be exacerbated by their exclusion from lifelong learning. It is bad if these young people leave school at 16 with no formal qualifications, but it is even worse if their capacity to *learn how to learn* is impaired, for the gap between them and those who are retained in formal education and training will then inevitably widen. Closing this gap means that the task of making *learning how to learn* an entitlement for all students has to become a central issue in the design of assessment as well as curriculum.

In short, in a school system that is so dominated by formal tests and examinations, from key stage one through to entry to higher education, both teachers and students develop an *instrumental* attitude to what they do, and this is undermining true education and the prerequisites of lifelong learning – the capacity and motivation to learn.

How do the critics respond to this state of affairs? Conservative critics argue that the teachers, along with the rest of the education establishment, including ministers and even the Prime Minister, have gone 'soft', that they are creating a world of 'prizes for all', where no student can fail, and that one of the functions of education is to give young people some experience of failure, which is one of life's realities. The logic of this position would be to scrap the D to G grades and turn them into an explicit fail mark. Indeed, such critics suggest that the GCSE and A-levels be recalibrated to ensure that fewer pass, particularly at the higher grades, thus resurrecting a strictly norm-referenced system to replace the (ostensibly) criterion-referenced system. For such critics the purpose of A-level is not to provide recognition of what students have achieved in their studies but to do the work of higher education institutions in enabling them to choose those most worthy of acceptance on a degree course.

Radical critics say that we have to find a positive way of recording achievement below level 2 or grades A to C or even abolish the GCSE completely. They believe that in accepting the status quo teachers are being compliant with an assessment system that has fundamental design faults. Recalling the success with which English teachers once forced a Secretary of State, John Patten, to back down on his assessment proposals, such critics would favour a professional rebellion to force change.

Many teachers do not align themselves fully with either the conservative or radical lines of argument. They acknowledge that the present system has real strengths, but they also recognise some fundamental faults that they claim could be easily remedied by ministers without overturning the whole assessment system − for it is ministers who have pushed what was once a reasonable system to breaking point by policies that have deformed it. While most teachers are convinced that currently assessment is excessive, they argue that several policy decisions, all reversible, also contribute to the crisis in assessment.

First, the setting of well-publicised *targets* for teachers in terms of the results in national key stage tests and the GCSEs/A-levels is forcing teachers to teach to the test and distort their practices.

Second, the test and examinations results are published in the form of *league tables* which have a huge impact on the school's reputation and affect parental choice, and so on student numbers and the school's income. These tables, many teachers say, give a misleading and unfair account of a school's achievement, because of the narrowness of what they measure and failure to take account of the character of a school's student intake.

Third, teachers' performance and pay is becoming increasingly linked to the performance of their students in tests and examinations, which adds yet further to the pressures that distort educational practices and induce stress in teachers. The longer ministers delay in changing policy, teachers say, the more the profession generally will lose any ownership of assessment, with which, unlike teachers everywhere else in the world, they apparently cannot be trusted. Moreover, a disturbing indicator of what is going awry is the teachers and head teachers with hitherto unblemished careers who are now being caught in various forms of malpractice aimed at getting better test and examination results. Growing numbers of teachers whose lives are tragically ruined in this way tell us that something is wrong.

Finally, the sheer cost of all these tests and examinations is out of proportion to their value, even if one ignores the costs of teachers' time that is now spent in preparing students for these assessments.

Ministers have shown a few signs of willingness to backtrack on any of these three T's − targets, tests and (league) tables − as well as performance-related pay.

A glimmer of light is the decision made in England – under the unacknowledged influence of Wales and fear of not reaching government targets – that key stage two targets should be set by teachers, rather than imposed from outside. Ministers continue to maintain that these are:

- essential levers in raising the performance of schools and teachers, which is central to improving the education service;
- necessary tools in monitoring the performance of schools and teachers; and part of a proper accountability of schools and the teaching profession to the public in general and in particular to parents, who like to be informed about tests results for their own children as well as the general performance of the local schools to provide the information that contributes to their choice of school;
- just measures for rewarding good teachers and effective incentives to improve the quality of teaching.

They see no obvious alternatives to achieving these aims and so believe any costs are justified by the benefits.

We thus reach the current terrible stalemate, in which neither side will concede much of the other side's case or come up with a solution that meets the other's concerns. So what is the way forward? The present system is so complex that there has always been the possibility of a disaster scenario, as has happened in Scotland and Northern Ireland. Some hoped something similar would happen in England too, as potentially the only way to bring ministers to their knees and force reform. It did happen in England in the summer of 2002 over the results for the very first cohort to complete the new A-level requirements, introduced two years earlier as Curriculum 2000. It did not, however, cause the system to collapse. Through the Tomlinson enquiry and the 14-19 Working Group he now chairs, a way to reform was opened, including possibilities, such as increased teacher assessment, that up to this point ministers had firmly ruled out. The remit of the Tomlinson Working Group excludes the national test system that ends at key stage three. It does not at this stage seem likely that there will be a unified formal assessment system for the whole of the school years, or even for the secondary phase. It would be unfortunate if the opportunity to return to first principles were to be missed amid the ministerial concern to patch up a flawed system and restore public confidence.

It will be some time before it becomes clear to what degree ministers will yield to pressure for reform and accept that the assessment systems need to be fundamentally reviewed and redesigned. The way forward demands that we consider the purposes and functions of our assessment systems and persuade the various partners to agree on which of them should have priority. The arguments deriving from a philosophy of lifelong learning have not been central in possible solutions to the weakness of our assessment systems, although they have a powerful contribution to make to deciding what actions need to be taken by the different partners to implement the agreed priorities.

The four purposes of a national assessment were set out in the Secretary of State's remit to the Qualifications and Curriculum Authority as:

- reporting on the attainment of individual pupils;
- monitoring national performance;
- contributing to the improvement of teaching and learning;
- contributing to the monitoring of the effectiveness of schools.

It is perhaps significant that improving teaching and learning is not at the head of this list, a position occupied, not surprisingly, by what the individual learner is achieving. Parents certainly have the right to know how their children are achieving at school and in a way that allows them to make a comparison with other children of the same age or key stage. From the perspective of lifelong learning, however, it must be the improvement of learning that is the highest priority and while reporting on each student's attainment is important, *it must be done in a way that contributes to the improvement of teaching and learning*. This is not easy to achieve, for getting feedback on high achievement can induce complacency in the learner (and the teacher too), and feedback on low achievement can induce a sense of failure and reduce motivation in the learner (and again in the teacher also). As we shall see, there may be ways of avoiding these unwanted side-effects of summative assessment.

It is the use of test and examination results to monitor national performance and school effectiveness that is the source of conflict between ministers and teachers. It is not, in fact, necessary to test every child at the end of a given key stage in order to monitor national trends in achievement: this could be done on the basis of a sample of some ten or twenty per cent of schools. Ministers insist on the publication of league tables on the grounds that this is a necessary form of local accountability, especially to parents in their choice of school. In reality, however, the data on school performance in any *one* year are not reliable, mainly because of variations in students' characteristics between years: information on school performance would be more accurate if based on an average of three years' results, and then presented in a 'value-added' form that takes account of student intake and prior achievement. Ministers would lose little if anything by such a change, but the gain from the goodwill of the profession feeling more fairly treated would be considerable. League tables devised on such a basis would certainly be more acceptable.

Moreover if ministers really wanted to inform parents as fully as is possible, they would devise a unified assessment system rather than the dual system that now exists – one system for key stages one to three, based on a particular set of levels, and another system devised for GCSE, AS- and A-levels, based on a different set of levels or grades. The various grades and levels, numbers and letters, seem to be designed to confuse. It is very difficult for parents or students to chart progression in learning over these two different systems, and especially at the transition point between systems during key stage four, when students' motivations and perceptions of the value of formal education are, like their self-identities, in a critical state of formation.

The costs of national assessment could be reduced quite considerably by a combination of two changes. More tests should be computer marked. One advantage is that more tests could be taken when the student is ready, rather than at a fixed time in the year, and this would also allow more rapid feedback to students and teachers, and thus potentially boost motivation. If the Secondary Heads Association's scheme for 'chartered examiners' were introduced, this would reduce the heavy costs of examinations by the diminution in external marking. A chartered examiner would be an experienced teacher who is trained and accredited to examine in a subject. A large department in a secondary school would have several chartered examiners to oversee rigorous internal marking and to be available to do similar work in a small school that lacks an accredited examiner. This could reduce the need for the external moderation to maintain standards. Following the 2002 A-level fiasco, there is interest from the government in the notion of chartered examiners, although this seems to be more motivated by the threat of a severe shortage of examiners than by what such a change might do to improve teachers' assessment skills.

It is widely recognised that we must increase the post-16 participation rate. The greatest obstacle to this is the notion that 16 is a natural school leaving age, reinforced by the very existence of the GCSE. In recent times there have been frequent calls for the abolition of the GCSE, and not just from teachers. The problem with such a course is that this would leave nothing in terms of qualifications or progress checks at this stage. A more prudent course is to retain the GCSE but make it less significant without reducing quality (that is, 'dumbing down'). This can be achieved by keeping external assessment only for the core subjects of English, Mathematics and Science, and having all other subjects assessed through chartered examiners and (light) external moderation. Further, students should be encouraged to take GCSEs early, that is, when ready, rather than at 16, and even skip them – as more now do each year – if they serve no particular purpose. Even better, the target of five GCSEs at grades A★ to C could be changed to GCSEs A★ to C in the core subjects of English, Mathematics and Science, which the government rightly recognises as the subjects that are vital to progression whatever the student chooses to do next. Remember that by no means all of those who get five A★ to C grades include all three core subjects in their achievement.

Such changes would not reduce the sense of failure among those students achieving D to G grades. There are too many grades, reflecting a well-intended but technically unjustified attempt to make very fine distinctions. In reality there are three working grades: the A★ and A grades; then the B and C grades, which make up the remainder of a level 2 qualification; and then D to G, which are level 1 and below the former O-level pass. It would be sensible to turn these into three actual grades, named in more positive terms, as distinction (A), credit (B and C), and pass (D to G). This will be of particular importance if the change from GNVQ, which had such a simple and positive grading structure, to the new GCSEs in vocational subjects is not to fail. Moreover it is essential to acknowledge that a single award, the GCSE, does not need to be restricted to a single assessment model: different subjects are more adequately and fairly assessed by methods that are fit for purpose rather than simply the same. In the longer term, there could be separate level 1 and level 2 units available across the whole of key stages three and four. Decreasing the significance of the GCSE would mean that the burden of assessment on students in three successive years – GCSE in year 11, AS in year 12 and A2 in year 13 – would be reduced.

Making the GCSE less of a 'high stakes' examination – for the student, for the teacher and for the school – is an essential condition for removing the unintended negative and distortive effects of this examination.

A second important benefit of the chartered examiner scheme is that it would improve the skills of all teachers in assessment, and this would underpin the most promising change in creating an assessment system that directly contributes to better teaching and learning, namely the widespread use of *assessment for learning* (AfL), or what used to be called 'formative assessment'. AfL is not just about giving feedback on learning for, as noted above, simple feedback can induce complacency ('your essay was brilliant') or helplessness ('your homework is a disgrace'). AfL is a process of identifying what the learner has or has not achieved *in order to plan the next steps in learning*. It looks forward to later learning rather than backwards. It is a process of providing feedback on student performance, but in such a way that *either* the teacher adjusts the teaching to help the student learn more effectively *or* the learner changes the approach to the learner task, *or* both of these.

So AfL is crucially about maximising motivation to learn and inducing in the learner the skills of *learning how to learn*. Through AfL the student:

- comes to hold a concept of the quality of a good performance that is similar to that held by the teacher, thus internalising the teacher's standard against which performance is judged;
- monitors his/her own performance so that it can be compared with this standard;
- is able to see how the performance can be improved, that is, engages in the action that closes the gap between performance and standard and thereby learns how to learn better.

No assessment system can ignore 'summative assessment' – the marks and grades that the learner attains at various points or the level needed to earn a qualification. But our present system is dominated so heavily by the summative that the formative AfL is in constant danger of being squeezed out. From the perspective of lifelong learning, AfL becomes the priority precisely because it helps students to *learn how to learn* and the summative is put into its proper place. Standards of student achievement have been rising, and they have done so under a government regime that has emphasised the summative. They will not continue to rise at the rate that is needed, especially in an education service that is more inclusive, retaining the lower achievers and those from the lower socioeconomic groups after 16, simply by more of the same. Raising standards means a new approach to assessment, one that puts AfL at the centre of a strategy of transformation that focuses on teaching and learning.

It is now clear that some modifications in the way the four purposes of national assessment set out by the Secretary of State are implemented could improve our assessment system. But if the object is to ensure that assessment actively supports students in acquiring the capacity and motivation for lifelong learning, then a fifth purpose must be added to the other four, so the list would read as follows:

- contributing to every learner's capacity and motivation to engage in lifelong learning;
- contributing to the improvement of teaching and learning;
- reporting on the attainment of individual pupils;
- monitoring national performance;
- contributing to monitoring the effectiveness of schools.

Here might be the most powerful driver of the deeper reform of our assessment systems, to ensure that fresh assessment policies and practices support rather than damage the skills of lifelong learning for all.

Does this all add up to making deep changes in the way teachers teach?

FOUR

Pedagogy

What matters is not the facts but how you discover and think about them: education in the true sense, very different from today's assessment-mad exam culture. (Richard Dawkins)

Apprenticeship may well be the means of instruction that builds most effectively on the ways in which most young people learn. (Howard Gardner)

To what degree teaching is (or could be) an art or a science or a combination of the two is a matter of deep dispute among teacher educators. Most practitioners in their classrooms would probably think of what they know and are able to do as principally an art, one they have acquired over many years, largely alone, through trial and error learning. Few would be able to cite any research evidence, except in the most general terms, to warrant what they do, although many educational researchers claim their influence on practising teachers is real, if rarely explicitly acknowledged.

What today is not in dispute is that if students are to become better learners, it is essential for teachers to become better at what they do. The dispute is about precisely *how* improving teaching quality is best achieved. Part of the trouble is that we know far more about learning than we do about teaching. This is in part because learning is of interest to a wide range of people apart from those who train teachers – psychologists, neuroscientists, cognitive scientists, anthropologists, and so on. In part it is because in a knowledge economy learning matters to many outside educational institutions, and especially those in business and industry, although here the talk is more likely to be of *mentoring* rather than teaching. *Teachers* and *teaching* are terms most people associate with schools and other explicitly educational institutions, and the people who study and research into teaching are therefore mainly those who prepare novice teachers and support the further professional development of career teachers.

Methods of teaching in schools as part of paid, professional activity – what we here call *pedagogy* – tends to be cut off from more 'natural' forms of teaching or what is thought of as *helping to learn*, whether in the workplace (for example, on-the-job learning with the support of a *mentor*) or in the home (for example, mothers' actions that assist the development of the infant) or in the community (for example, what the young learn from their peers). It is vitally important to study and understand learning and teaching wherever they occur. This is not helped by the fact that those who teach but are not school teachers prefer not to call themselves teachers at all: in colleges and universities teachers often prefer the term *tutor* or *lecturer*, and in the workplace or on the sports field, terms such as *mentor* or *coach* are the norm.

Fortunately, one of the most important characteristics of human beings is that *we are programmed to learn*. The scientific evidence is clear. Babies are born as brilliantly intelligent learners. It is incredible how much they learn so easily and quickly when they are very young. They are profoundly motivated to learn by using the powerful abilities with which they are by nature endowed. As Alison Gopnik and her fellow psychologists explain:

> Babies begin by translating information from the world into rich, complex, abstract, coherent representations. Those representations allow babies to interpret their experience in particular ways and to make predictions about new events. Babies are born with powerful programs already booted up and ready to run. Their experiences lead babies and young children to enrich, modify, revise, reshape, reorganise, and sometimes replace their initial representations, and so end up with other, quite different rich, complex, abstract, coherent representations. As children take in more input from the world, their rules for translating, manipulating, and rearranging that input also change. Rather than having a single program, they have a succession of progressively more powerful and accurate programs. Children themselves play an active role in this process by exploring and experimenting. Children reprogram themselves. Other people, especially those who take care of children, naturally act in ways that promote and influence the changes in children's representations and rules. Mostly they do this quite unconsciously. Other people are programed to help children reprogram themselves.

We seem to be less rigidly programmed than other creatures to engage in highly specific behaviours in an automatic or instinctive way: we have powerful propensities, for language acquisition for instance, but our brains are sufficiently plastic to enable us to master the specific language(s) of our culture quickly and easily. Lifelong learning, then, is natural to humans in a far stronger form than in other creatures. True, as we get older we are often less plastic than when young: it is much harder to pick up a second or third language after puberty. It is also true that we may pick up poor habits or techniques of learning. Nevertheless, we can and do learn very successfully throughout life. Older humans are able to learn new tricks in a way that is utterly impossible for dogs.

Any education system should trade on this powerful learning capacity. It is, however, a disconcerting fact that by the time they have reached the end of compulsory schooling, about a third of young people have been turned off formal learning, most of whom have a strong sense of failure. They have learned little, which is bad enough. Even worse, however, is the fact that their inborn capacity to learn has also been damaged. This is caused by many factors, including some approaches to curriculum and assessment, as already discussed. How learners are taught can both prevent learning and damage learning capacity.

Learning is often described as the *acquisition of knowledge, skill and understanding*. Chris Woodhead, the former Chief Inspector, was once asked by Jeremy Paxman in a broadcast interview to describe the role of the teacher. Woodhead's answer was: *to tell*. Paxman paused for Woodhead to continue, but surprisingly he did not. He has made the same point in print. "Good teachers", he insists, "tell you things. That should be the end of the story".

This is perversely simplistic and irresponsibly dangerous. Telling – instructing, lecturing – is undoubtedly one strand of teaching. While its significance has declined over the last century as learners have had greater access to the material in other, often more attractive forms, there are still many occasions when it is essential for teachers to tell their students something. But it is no more than one of the many means teachers adopt to achieve the end of teaching, which is, of course, that the learner should learn. The better the teacher, the more varied and sophisticated is the repertoire of strategies that can be deployed to engage the student in learning and to enjoy the pleasures it brings.

Teaching-as-telling reinforces the folk psychology of teaching that learning is simply the acquisition, mainly through processes of memorisation, of stuff called knowledge or facts. For pupils, learning is 'work' that involves the effort of memorising what is often perceived as not worth remembering. Yet they have little trouble committing to memory the things that really matter to them and so doing is by no means regarded as work. Thus it comes about that students develop a distinctive perspective on learning and education, neatly captured by John Holt:

> For children, the business of school is not learning, whatever this vague word means; it is getting these daily tasks done, or at least out of the way, with a minimum of effort and unpleasantness. Each task is an end in itself. The children don't care how they dispose of it. If they can get it out of the way by doing it, they will do it; if experience has taught them this does not work very well, they will turn to other, illegitimate means, that wholly defeat whatever purpose the teacher may have had in mind. (Holt, 1964)

Moreover, learning involves more than acquiring knowledge, skill and understanding. A good, rather than minimally adequate, education system will *enhance* our capacity to learn. This is what *learning how to learn* is about. Here is the essence of lifelong learning. Pedagogy should at its best be about what teachers do that not only helps students to learn but actively strengthens their capacity to learn.

There is, then, a duality in the teacher's role and we must distinguish different kinds of learning. One kind, the everyday definition, is the acquisition of knowledge, skill and understanding. *Learning how to learn* (or meta-learning) is another kind. The conventional term is something of a misnomer, in that we do not need to be taught how to learn; it is something we inherit as part of our programming. *Learning how to learn* is really about how a learner can be helped to learn more effectively than would occur naturally and without intervention. Part of this involves *meta-cognition*, the capacity to observe and change the ways in which we set about learning. Just as there is a content to learning (the subjects and disciplines that make a curriculum), there are different elements in meta-learning (a meta-curriculum of the actions that improve one's ability to learn). There are simple, well-established skills, such as mnemonics or simulations, newer approaches, such as research and evaluation skills, and 'thinking skills', about which there are different schools of thought. Others would express meta-learning as being concerned with 'creativity' or 'problem solving'. Such transferable *generic skills*, and their associated attitudes and dispositions, are assumed to be of vital importance in allowing people to learn effectively as they move from one situation, context or activity to another.

In the knowledge society, some (but by no means most) knowledge changes rapidly. There are now few occupations in which the knowledge and skill involved will remain unchanged for a lifetime. To be successful in a knowledge-based economy, learners not only have to learn, but also have to become more adept at learning so that it becomes a universal lifelong skill. Some questions arise:

- Do we know what is involved in meta-learning?
- Is it possible to teach a person how to learn more effectively?
- Should teachers teach their students to do so?
- If so, do they know how to do it?
- And if not, can they be taught how to teach meta-learning to their students?

The answer to all these questions is 'yes'. Our knowledge of meta-learning is as yet somewhat primitive, but is growing rapidly. Those with expertise in the area are not in agreement about the content of meta-learning, or even about the terms in which it is best described. Certainly these are not topics that teachers can talk about very easily. As Philip Jackson observed:

> One of the most notable features of teacher talk is the absence of a technical vocabulary. Unlike professional encounters between doctors, lawyers, mechanics and astrophysicists, when teachers talk together almost any reasonably intelligent adult can listen in and comprehend what is being said. (Jackson, 1968)

Teachers lack an agreed discourse for what they already know as part of the traditional culture and wisdom of the profession. This is not a demand for an arcane, pedagogic jargon: the technical language devised by academics is alien to most teachers. Yet the profession lacks a shared language that allows them to be clear and precise, so their vocabulary remains impoverished. They get by, of course, but the flaw is exposed when teachers talk about those aspects of teaching and learning that are new or difficult. Many of the teachers who developed assessment for learning with Black and Wiliam wanted their advice on the meaning of learning. The academic community in education has yet to provide teachers with an agreed working vocabulary about learning, despite it being the core concept of the teaching profession. Occasionally, academics have invented memorable classifications, such as Guy Claxton's (2000) ingenious and memorable five I's as ways of learning – through *immersion, imitation, imagination, intuition* and *intellect* – or his three generic R's – *resourcefulness, resilience* and *reflectiveness*.

There is evidence that meta-learning, like other ways of learning, can be taught, but most teachers have not themselves been trained how to teach meta-learning, and do not feel confident about doing it. As we shall see, to do so successfully often requires them to question some of their assumptions about their current professional practices.

If the argument in the earlier quotation from the psychologists is true, then we are programmed, at least to some degree, to help the young to learn successfully. They might do quite a lot unaided, but with adult support they learn much more effectively and efficiently. This adult help is offered *naturally*: we do not have to train people in how to do it. Schools, and professional teachers, are relatively recent creations in human beings' history. Do they make use of this natural knowledge about teaching and learning? Perhaps they do. But the young are surrounded by many under-exploited examples of natural teaching and learning from which they could profit. We must look with the eyes of an anthropologist, who treats the normal world as strange. The anthropologist looks more closely and with an enquiring eye, detecting details that escape the rest of us, and thereby providing unexpected explanations of what we have taken for granted as unquestioned. This is the origin of one of the most influential of modern theories of learning, called *situated learning*.

Jean Lave and Etienne Wenger are anthropologists who analysed studies of apprentices – midwives in Mexico, tailors in Liberia, and navy quartermasters, butchers and alcoholics in the US – from which they proposed a novel way of understanding learning. Apprentices want to become like their master: they are novices who want to become full members of a community of practice. They do this through a particular form of learning. At first they lack the knowledge and skill of the master and they participate in the community in a highly peripheral way. Over time, they move from the edge of the community as they are given more responsibility and progressively learn what it takes to be a member and practise the craft as a full participant. There is, however, little observable teaching of an explicit, conventional kind. The 'curriculum' is the practice of the community into which the apprentice is progressively initiated. A learning curriculum unfolds in the opportunities the master gives them for engaging to a partial extent in the practices of the community. Much learning will be achieved through observation and imitation. The apprentices are not thereby merely acquiring new knowledge and skills: they are being inducted into a culture that will eventually transform their identity and the way in which they define themselves.

Apprenticeship is the archetypal form of situated learning, the principles of which can be applied to many other contexts. In particular, some school contexts of learning, which are currently very unlike apprenticeships, could be adjusted to make better use of the principles of situated learning. Many young people would learn better if they were placed in authentic settings where the spontaneous, progressive learning and the 'teaching' of semi-conscious support provided by attentive adults occur as naturally as in apprenticeships. But schooling is, and in the short term will remain, a very different experience for most learners, who:

- do not wish to be like their teachers, who are not 'masters' in the usual sense and often lack the respect that is afforded by apprentices to their masters;
- are not joining, and learning to participate in, what they see as a desirable culture;
- lack motivation to acquire much of the knowledge and skill, which is fragmented and unrelated to their identity.

But it is possible that some vulnerable and school-averse young people – and this group is *not* synonymous with the 'less able' – could be helped to experience, part-time or full-time, such apprenticeship modes, either in a true apprenticeship or in substantial opportunities for work-related or work-based learning, or other attractive activities with non-teacher adults in the community, or places where the relationships are closer to that of master-apprentice than of classroom teacher-student. Many students need to get closer to adults with whom they identify as role models, and from whom they can learn that learning in un-school like ways is a natural, important and enjoyable part of their lives. Young people are surrounded by excellent, non-professional 'teachers' from every walk of life: the education service does not know how to value and use them to help the students to learn and learn how to learn.

There is thus a sharp contrast between 'doing an apprenticeship' and 'doing school'. In apprenticeship, much of the knowledge is 'know-how' which is very concrete but is more easily demonstrated than talked about. The knowledge is embedded in action and so is learned in a rather piecemeal way through on-the-job practice. It is built up through experience and rehearsal, but once mastered is forgotten very slowly. In 'doing school', by contrast, the student is faced with knowledge mainly in the form of 'know-that', which is easily stated and acquired through speech or writing, but is remote from practical application. It is accumulated as a stack of information, rather than a stock of experience, that has to be committed to memory, rehearsed in revision, tested in written examinations, and then quickly forgotten. Doing school is not the most natural way of learning.

We know that apprentice-style or situated learning is difficult to provide within the conventional structure we call *the lesson*, but from the work of writers such as Tom Bentley (1998), Adria Steinberg (1998), Valerie Bayliss (1999) and Guy Claxton (2000), it evidently can be achieved in the very different structure of the *project*. The key features of projects can be listed as follows:

- The objectives of the activity are clearly defined, understood and subscribed to.
- The task is authentic: the problem to be solved is a real one.
- There is a clear and identifiable outcome or endpoint.
- The activity is challenging, requiring a wide range of skills, including generic skills, and disciplined thinking and behaviour.
- The activity requires the learner to participate actively and so to extend current competences or acquire new ones.
- The learner is given real responsibility and is required to make important decisions that have real consequences for the self, for the task and for other people.
- The tasks demand the use of real resources, materials that have to be sought out or created and then used.
- The activity takes some time to complete, requires careful planning; and entails making some mistakes.
- Help and support is needed from adults with experience of the activity and who are willing to serve as *mentors*.
- Adult–learner relationships differ from conventional teacher–student styles.
- There are opportunities to observe and imitate experienced adults.
- There are opportunities for independent learning that fosters the culture of self-education and the autodidact.
- Learners work in teams and act as *mentors* to one another.
- Learners get feedback on what they do, on both success and failure.
- Success is celebrated on completion of the activity.

Now if we take these as criteria of what would make a good learning activity in school, the truth is that most of the diet of schools fails to meet the majority, not just some, of these criteria. That is why, as John Holt (1964) noted, that from the learners' point of view, most lessons consists of tasks that they have to get through and be rid of.

By contrast, the learning that a well-designed *project* sustains is far more like the natural learning of the infant and the learning of adults in their daily lives. Yet projects of this kind are rarely provided for students in the routine of school life. Of course not all project work in schools displays these features. Indeed, project work in primary schools got a bad name because too often it lacked these features. Projects have tended to be squeezed out of both primary and secondary schools. The project needs to be rehabilitated, not abandoned. There are more opportunities for project-like activities and *mentor* roles for teachers than appear at first sight. Teachers of physical education, music tutors and art and design teachers have an expertise in mentoring and coaching that is rarely recognised by their colleagues. The American psychologist Ann Brown has shown that it is possible to create in the primary classroom what she called 'communities of inquiry' which are in many ways a replica among pupils of Lave and Wenger's 'communities of practice' in the adult world. We clearly need some bold experiments to develop robust projects that last for a day, a week or even a year (for instance, a Year 11 that acts as a break between GCSEs taken early in Year 10 and the beginning of A-level courses in Year 12). There are, I suspect, few innovations more likely to enhance student motivation and enjoyment in learning, not least because there is an end-product that is more than a qualification or an exam pass. Teachers who have produced plays and music festivals understand why, to the student participants, these events are among the most treasured memories of school. Yet we keep such events at the periphery, in the *extra*-curriculum, where they cannot challenge or contaminate the sacred timetable of countless short lessons in which it is virtually impossible to achieve the characteristics of the worthwhile *project*. Nor are they allowed to challenge the 'normal' relationships between teachers and taught in ordinary classrooms.

The constraints of buildings and the structure of the school day militate against project work, especially in secondary education, as we shall explore later. In these circumstances, a more common approach to teaching meta-learning is the special lesson dedicated to providing students with strategies for improving their learning. As noted earlier, there are various approaches to the teaching of 'thinking skills' and creativity. Students can also be helped to learn better, through guided reflection on their learning style or by assessing the quality of their work. The assumption is that what is learned can be transferred to 'ordinary' lessons – and experience of earlier attempts to improve 'study skills' suggests that this assumption may not always be warranted. Nevertheless, it is clear that in the absence of such interventions many students rarely think about their own thinking or acquire new or better strategies for learning.

Many teachers, however, may be reluctant to allocate time to such meta-learning activities on the grounds that they need all the available time for conventional teaching and learning. Such teachers want a *high leverage* method of teaching meta-learning. Leverage is concerned with the relationship between the energy and effort of the teacher's input in relation to the quality of the student outcome. A low leverage strategy is one where the teacher has to make a high input for a very small difference in student outcome; most teachers are familiar with this. A high leverage strategy is one where the teacher input is relatively small, but the student outcome is high.

The question is this: are there high leverage strategies for meta-learning? The work of Dylan Wiliam and Paul Black on *assessment for learning*, as reported in the last chapter, suggests that there are. Two routine practices of teachers are asking questions of students and marking their work with grades. Potentially both strategies can support meta-learning.

When students are asked questions, particularly open rather than closed ones, they potentially have to think hard about the problem, re-work existing knowledge or apply it to a novel situation. After asking a question, most teachers leave very little time for the student to answer before moving on to someone else. When asked, teachers say they think they wait for several seconds, but in fact they rarely wait for more than two seconds. Teachers have probably come to adopt a very short wait time for they fear a longer period of silence for thinking will create an opportunity for distraction or deviance. So they end up asking closed questions, reinforcing in the pupils' minds the misleading notion that learning is only a matter of memorising what can be recalled and reproduced in the tests and examinations that now loom so large for students as well as teachers. The normal wait time is too short, especially when we remember that the more challenging the question – as opposed to the closed questions where the teacher is just checking what the students know – the more cognitive work from the pupil is required. If students lack sufficient time to think, then they keep quiet or offer a thoughtless answer, which defeats the point of the questioning. Teachers can – with some effort – increase their wait time and so provoke more frequent and/or higher quality answers. A decent wait time is essential for serious thinking and learning by students, and for changing their crude conceptions of the very meaning of learning.

In a similar way, Black and Wiliam have shown that if teachers do not put grades or marks on student work, students increase their attention to the comments and suggestions made by the teacher. Grades simply tell students that they have done well (a high mark) or badly (a low mark), both of which serve as a terminal switch-off against further thinking or learning. Comments and suggestions support student reflection on strengths and weaknesses and what they might do to improve their learning. The difficult part, of course, may be persuading teachers to resist their long-standing inclination to grade student work, a practice that is encouraged by many assessment schemes.

Most radically of all, Black and Wiliam have revealed the meta-learning that can be aroused in students when they are asked to assess their own work and that of other students, having to justify their judgements and even devise their own mark schemes. When students learn how to set good questions, they have demonstrated both mastery of the topic and what must be done to demonstrate the quality of the learning. Meta-learning can be taught to students with demonstrable beneficial effects on ordinary learning and thus on achievement.

In short, the work on assessment for learning helps to solve the riddle of how one teaches *learning how to learn* and *generic skills* without demanding more curriculum time and so squeezing curriculum content. It is that both *learning how to learn* and *generic skills* are taught not directly as separate subjects, demanding additional time and a place on the timetable, but rather they are taught *through* much conventional content by a shift in pedagogy, or the way the content is taught. Moreover, the *project* is precisely a way of organising teaching and learning that supports such a pedagogy and ensures that *learning how to learn* and *generic skills* can be mastered by students.

These examples show that to teach meta-learning and to see the content of the curriculum as constructed around *projects* rather than conventional *lessons*, teachers have to question their own assumptions and practices. There is much to commend the notion of 'extended school', but its potential will not be fully exploited if it becomes merely more of the same or even different for no particular reason or purpose. Initiatives such as this should be taken as opportunities to develop the notion of the *project* and to find ways in which such innovations can penetrate back into the organisation of the conventional school day and the way in which teachers teach.

Teachers need to become learners and meta-learners too. This brings both teachers and students to the heart of the challenge of lifelong learning, for teachers need to be models of the qualities that underpin lifelong learning in knowledge economies. Imitation is one of the most basic, and currently most neglected, drivers of learning: teachers abandon imitation to the vagaries of the peer group. In some (but not all) of their work, teachers need the authority that derives from an *intellectual mastery* of their subject, without which they never acquire the equally essential, but very different, authority that derives from the skill of *teaching* the subject successfully. Hitherto this has been enough for teachers to enjoy professional success. Today, however, teachers have to transmit to their students both the will to learn and the belief that they can learn better: all students should leave school as motivated and competent learners. They must, in short, be like the natural, good learners that they were in the first three years of life. The powerful early programming for intensive learning runs down with age: in the knowledge-based economy, where more and more work depends on the ability to learn and to apply knowledge, we have to find a means of maintaining, through the successful teaching of meta-learning through projects, what education at its best bestows on students, this motivation to study and capacity to learn. This is the pedagogic challenge of lifelong learning.

As students make more choices in what they learn, and these choices have significant long-term consequences, do they receive enough advice and guidance?

FIVE

Advice and guidance

A good educational system should have three purposes: it should provide all who want to learn with access to available resources at any time in their lives; empower all who want to share what they know to find those who want to learn it from them; and, finally, furnish all who want to present an issue to the public with the opportunity to make their challenge known. (Ivan Illich)

Career guidance is being subordinated to the government's social inclusion agenda. The importance of career guidance in supporting its 14-19 curriculum reforms and its skills agenda is being lost, as is its role in reducing drop-out in further and higher education due to ill-informed and ill-thought-through choices. The focus is merely on engagement and retention, not on successful transition and progression. (Tony Watts)

Who needs to provide educational advice and guidance to whom on what matters and for what purposes? What contribution could and should this make to lifelong learning? Does lifelong learning entail a rethinking of educational advice and guidance?

In the emerging knowledge-based economy, many have argued, a career as we have known it, that is, an occupation that is entered at a point between the mid-teens and mid-twenties and not left until retirement some 30 to 40 years later, is in many cases in decline. Steady work – being able to continue in the same job for a predictable level of pay – is disappearing for all but a minority of working people, says Robert Reich (1991), the former US Secretary of Labor. New rules of employment, claims William Bridges (1995), are emerging. In a turbulent environment, organisations rapidly succeed or die, so employment is contingent on employees demonstrating their continuing value to the organisation. Employees become more like independent business agents who sell services to an employer, which means generating a self-development plan that includes the capacity to re-educate and re-design oneself as well as taking primary responsibility for investing for healthcare and a pension. In the workplace, the skill of the project worker and manager are at a premium and ease the movement from one organisation to another. The evidence in the UK indicates that the shift away from permanent, full-time and lifelong jobs is real, although the rate of shift has been exaggerated. If the trend continues there will be an increase in Charles Handy's 'portfolio' workers whose complex career patterns have not been common in the careers advice and guidance services provided in schools and colleges. Such services are less and less a 'one-off' occasion on which a young person is helped to choose a lifetime career and given advice on the necessary first steps, and more and more an education into the rapidly changing world of work for which advice and guidance, and recurrent education and training, will be needed throughout life for a substantial portion of the population.

Traditionally advice and guidance in education has been associated with work and careers, and has therefore been offered to help in the choice of courses and qualifications, and very often directed to young people about to leave school or university to enter the world of work. In recent times, some of these services in England have been brought under the umbrella of the Connexions service, created as an outcome of a report by the Social Exclusion Unit. Careers guidance has usually been most heavily addressed to students who leave school at the earliest opportunity to take up employment or a combination of work and training. The Unit was particularly concerned with those at risk of disengagement and unemployment (and so often the lowest achievers) and the remit and design of the Connexions service has been shaped by the needs of this category of client. At the time, the New Labour government was committed to 'joined-up' provision of services as a means to their improvement, so Connexions was planned as a horizontally integrated model, bringing together the various strands of information, advice and guidance (IAG) for a particular age group and especially for what is undoubtedly the most vulnerable or 'at-risk' sub-group.

This is, perhaps, a strange time in which to design in England a horizontally integrated system, with its undoubted merits, despite serious criticism from professional and practitioner quarters, rather than a vertically integrated, lifelong IAG system, as is being developed in Wales and Scotland. The government's action was in part influenced by the fact that the careers budget was the only one it could directly control. Targeting the resources at the minority of young people 'at-risk' means, however, that the same kind of service cannot be extended to the rest of the population, many of whom will need – in the quite new category or sense of being 'at-risk' being described by Reich, Bridges and Handy – information, advice and guidance in forms and with a regularity that were quite unnecessary to their educational equivalents of a generation ago.

Moreover, the very concept of 'personal adviser', so central to Connexions, is under critical scrutiny. Certainly the vulnerable will fare better when the various forms of help are provided by just the one person, who establishes a strong and enduring relationship with the young client. How easy it will be to maintain such a consistent relationship over an extended period is open to doubt, particularly in inner-city areas, where both 'at-risk' adolescents *and* geographically mobile professionals, such as advisers and teachers, are to be found in disproportionate numbers. Moreover it is arguable that the complexity of the services to be offered is more likely to be met by a team, including a careers adviser, than by a hard-to-find, multi-skilled polymath. There is thus considerable scope for the personal adviser to act as a broker. It is the latter that many see as the more realistic role definition to offer the best services to those who may later become portfolio workers in knowledge economies.

Careers education and guidance in schools is also in need of reformulation. Only a third of the teachers who have the status of the careers coordinator have a recognised qualification in the field and about half are insufficiently trained. In school, they have relatively little timetable time. Careers education and guidance is allocated, on average, less than six hours per year in Years 7 and 8, just over twice this in Year 9, and 20-22 hours in Years 10 and 11. The new arrangements for greater flexibility in key stage four mean that in Year 9 students will now make more choices of a more consequential kind, especially over vocationally related options and the new GCSEs in vocational subjects: *all* students and their parents now need more information and advice than ever before.

The test of careers education and guidance may well depend on the successful preparation of young people, not simply in matters of immediate or direct relevance to employment or qualifications as such, but rather in the development of skills of self-diagnosis and self-management that are of general value in life, and now assume a new significance in relation to work. Drawing up plans, evaluating options, making decisions, managing transitions, are the kinds of skill that underpin employment from the earliest period, and certainly key stage three. There are few indications that such skills are being given any priority, despite their potential for the enrichment of the meta-learning discussed in the last chapter. Happily the new careers education and guidance framework issued by the DfES gives the school a welcome responsibility here. But without more, and better qualified, careers coordinators who work in explicit partnership with careers advisers in Connexions, the school-based systems will remain weak and inadequate for the task.

The reality is that advice and guidance so often comes from those who know far too little for the task: ordinary teachers who advise on, and deeply influence, students' choices of subject options; parents who have strong views based on their own direct experience and who may well blindly insist that their children follow academic courses as the preferred, prestige route in education; and peers with their short-term perspectives and pressures to 'follow the crowd'. Non-specialised teachers, parents and friends are often profoundly ignorant of current and predicted local labour markets, despite their obvious importance to career choices, and few teachers (but rather more parents) have direct experience of portfolio working. Hence the importance of careers advisers and coordinators. Parents and teachers should be allies of careers advisers, rather than the source of competing advice: how much IAG time and energy should be given to working with parents and teachers, rather than directly with students, is an interesting question.

Understanding of work and qualifications would be also greater if the National Qualifications Framework, currently under review, were simpler and better known. Part of the problem is the fear of devising an easy-to-follow map of the main pathways that might be interpreted in a simplistic way in the conventional terms of 'academic' and 'vocational': the divisive tripartite system of half a century ago continues to haunt us. We seem to be trapped by widespread beliefs that 'vocational' means second class and non-intellectual, and is to be contrasted with the concept of 'professional', which is linked to academic pathways and higher education. So the clients for the careers coordinator are the parents and colleague teachers as much as the students: unless all are much better informed than now there is little hope of a change in public perceptions of employment and qualifications.

The irony is that better advice and guidance may be crucial to what is now central to the government's educational agenda, namely increasing the post-16 participation rate. England is currently near the bottom of the OECD league table on post-16 retention, just ahead of Mexico, Greece and Turkey – this is not a position in which we take pride. Schools and colleges will be under growing pressure to keep young people in education and training after the age of 16, but such participation is only of value if students find themselves on courses of study that meet two criteria: first, they make sense to young people as a route to further education and employment; and second, the course must be of sufficient quality that the choice of it gives real satisfaction to students. Otherwise we shall continue to have a high drop-out rate among disenchanted 17-year-olds who feel the system has led them astray.

It is often forgotten that the majority of post-16 students are *not* in schools, but in colleges (where guidance may be restricted to which of the college's courses to take) and/or workplaces (where there may be no guidance at all). The colleges are grossly under-resourced in terms of personnel able to give high quality advice and guidance at what is a critical period for many young people. As a result, too many students, confused by the welter of qualifications, drift into inappropriate but bureaucratically convenient institutional 'slots', that lack educational coherence and progression. It is to be hoped that the Tomlinson Working Group will recommend changes that result in a clearer structure of a smaller number of vocational qualifications of higher quality. The challenge for 14–19 reform is to redesign the system so that those most 'at-risk' do not fall out of the system at the age of 16 but also that those who continue to participate at 16 are able to make properly informed choices within a more flexible system that meets their needs better.

As part of their post-16 provision, students should begin to believe that they are now gaining regular access to an integrated IAG system that will potentially become a lifelong companion offering continuing support. But this entails being clearer about the purposes, content and value of a vocational course or qualification. For there are courses/qualifications that are vocationally relevant, providing an insight into a broad vocational area and giving a taste of what employment in that field might entail; and there are occupational qualifications, which do prepare young people for a specific occupation, as well as apprenticeships. I suspect too many young people end up with a qualification that seems relevant to a vocation but contains little of the knowledge and skills that employers believe are needed to do the job. We need a system that allows a young person to explore a vocational area without longer commitment and then, if the initial choice turns out to be a mistake, to withdraw and look elsewhere. At the same time, when the young person's occupational choice becomes clear, then the qualification must have the explicit support of relevant employers. It is too easy in post-16 education to offer young people courses that seem interesting to them – such as performing arts and media studies – and that hint at possible careers but are very unlikely to lead to them.

Careers education and guidance in school becomes a more important element in overall provision, but remains at the margins of the curriculum. It seems unlikely that this will change until there is a larger and more radical re-consideration of the 'non-subject' parts of the curriculum. In recent years, careers education has moved closer to personal, social and health education (PSHE) in its emphasis on the development of the skills of self-management and independent functioning. The changing nature of employment now demands navigational skills that are relevant to the rest of life in complex societies. Indeed, the whole area is becoming more and more linked to various forms of meta-learning. The difficulty is that when the National Curriculum was being reviewed and revised at the turn of the last century, the main pressure was on the introduction of citizenship education. There was an understandable fear that this would become a weak addition to PSHE, without a clear identity, a defined content and a proper time allocation. The movement for citizenship education succeeded, but the opportunity was lost to re-think the broader area of PSHE, which remains a conceptual mess. From the point of view of the changing demands of the knowledge economy and urgency of better preparation for lifelong learning, the area that most needs some serious intellectual work to give it a new importance and status, remains uneasily and insecurely at the margins.

One hope on the horizon is the growing significance of *work-related learning*, the only new statutory requirement for key stage four in the government's 14-19 reforms. This is not another name for work experience or work shadowing or work-based learning or taster courses, although all these are relevant parts of it. It is a broader concept that includes giving young people some experience of work, of working practices and environments, and of skills in working life; and it especially involves the recognition that work is not the same as a *job* or a *career*. It can be achieved through the workplace or through activities that are work-related. Enterprise activities and entrepreneurial attitudes and skills are of particular importance here. The precise form that work-related learning takes will vary widely with the different needs and preferences of students in the light of the courses they follow. Potentially it is a new bridge between the academic and the vocational, between life in the institution of the school and life in the workplace and wider world. It remains to be seen whether this opportunity will be fully realised.

Although the relations between business and education are today much improved, there is still too little dialogue between employers and teachers about the qualities that are most valued in the workplace. Of course employers need young people with literacy, numeracy and information and communication technology (ICT) skills, but in many spheres of employment highly specific knowledge is not needed prior to entry to the workplace. There are important exceptions, of course, especially where a complex technical skill base, as in some areas of science and technology, is an essential prerequisite. But in a surprising number of jobs, even at graduate level, much of the knowledge acquired through formal education is of relatively low relevance. It has been shown that the work demands of the university student are very different from those of employment. For *the student-as-learner*, the tasks flow from pre-set educational objectives; the learning is highly explicit and focused on abstract intellectual problems deriving from a coherent intellectual framework. To solve these problems, the learner works largely alone, with introverted and isolated study habits: the learner is jealous and protective of personal research. Interpersonal skills and teamwork are not developed. As solutions to problems are found, they must be expressed in writing, the quality of which is judged by an expert.

For the *graduate-as-learner* in the workplace, the tasks arise in a less ordered and coherent way. The learning is more implicit and informal, acquired as problems are tackled in cost- and time-efficient ways. Lateral and critical thinking processes are likely to be needed, and solutions are reached through a mixture of self-evaluation and teamwork. The most effective worker has a high level of social skills, knows how to collaborate and is gregarious in work habits. These are not, however, the qualities needed by a successful university teacher (or schoolteacher, of course) and so they continue to be neglected in formal education. It may be that professional teachers in formal education develop lifelong skills and habits for formal learning, but not necessarily the skills and habit for lifelong learning in the worlds beyond educational institutions. If professional teachers often lack some of the core qualities that their students need for lifelong learning, then perhaps, as we shall discuss in Chapter Nine, this is an indictment of our conception of the teaching profession.

In short, the structure of work is much closer to the structure of the *project* than to the school lesson or the university course. The skills that are needed in work do not need to be taught through specifically vocational courses: it is the way that learning is organised and supported through pedagogy that ensures that students acquire the *generic skills* and *learning how to learn* that matter so much in life and in the workplace. The government's recent skills strategy – *21st century skills: Realising our potential* insists that education must do more to meet the needs of employers and accepts that they often want these generic skills. Yet it fails to elaborate on the implications for this, assigning the question of detail to the Tomlinson Working Group which will, we are told, take account of "the generic skills, attributes and knowledge essential to underpin progression, further learning, employment and adult life". There is a real danger in repeating the self-indulgent rhetoric that has failed to confront the issues of the place of generic skills in school-age education, which has characterised government pronouncements since the Confederation of British Industry's (CBI) seminal *Towards a skills revolution* published over a decade ago.

As these boundaries blur between what is IAG and what is work, education and training or just life, it is clear that IAG cannot be a centralised system. Nor should it be a series of government initiatives that are little known and rarely coordinated. The centre can, however, provide a framework in which the various specialised and strategic agencies – notably the Guidance Council, the Guidance Accreditation Board, the Federation of Professional Associations in Guidance and the National IAG Board – can work together successfully and with a wide range of partners in education, training and employment, as well as in other spheres of guidance, such as marriage guidance. The centre can also intervene to provide a UK-wide labour market information system that documents current skill levels, offers national and regional skill forecasts; lists job vacancies and training provision. Overall, however, integration here is a matter of coherence through cooperation rather than command and control. There will continue to be a need for professionals within that system – with its formal elements (that at some point have to be paid for from the public or private purse), but equally important informal aspects (universally accessible and largely free), led by well-informed families, friends, employers and teachers – but more as brokers of, and professional supports for, that system rather than its expert controllers.

One possibility here might be to examine the conceptual model underpinning the Health and Safety at Work Act of 1974 as a potential model for a national IAG framework. The IAG service should be organised and delivered within a coherent framework of enabling legislation that brings together all relevant, existing statutory provision. The legislation would articulate a fundamental change in the way the policy is conceptualised. IAG would be shaped around the process of learning and the status of the learner, in place of the current preoccupation with the content, timing and physical location of formal education and training. IAG would be developed as a range of more flexible, innovative options. Decisions about the form, content, timing and mode of delivery should be taken as close as possible to the site of opportunities and challenges as they occur.

The model involves only one general duty on the enforcing authorities, probably local education authorities (LEAs) and local Learning and Skills Councils (LSCs), to provide a coherent, standards-based range of IAG services on an all-age basis. A commission, appointed by the Secretary of State, should oversee the development and operation of the framework through powers to approve, and issue codes of practice and conduct investigations. An Executive would be responsible for enforcing the general duty and to that end would appoint and deploy a body of inspectors.

Such a development would be no more than a bridge to a deeper social reconstruction, one that has already been envisioned by a small number of writers. As long ago as 1971, Ivan Illich (1971) made the crucial insight that the nature of learning, and new tools for learning, would have to change concurrently with the quality and structure of daily life. His proposed new system had two purposes, ones that are at the foundation of lifelong learning: providing all who want to learn with access to the relevant resources at any time of life and empowering all who want to share their knowledge and experience to do so. These purposes, Illich argued, could be achieved through learning webs or networks – and remember this is a full 30 years ago – that he extrapolated from the telephone and postal services. He imagined four networks that would give access to the vast and underexploited educational resources embodied in things, models, peers and elders. The first network is a *reference service* to resources for formal learning – libraries, museums and so on; the second a *skill exchange* through which people list the knowledge and skills they are willing to offer to learners; the third a *peer-matching communications network* through which a learner finds partners; and the fourth a *directory of professional educators* or freelancers who offer services. This is surprisingly close to the kind of structure and framework of an IAG system, as discussed above, embedded within an educational service designed to support lifelong learning. Huge emphasis is placed on voluntary and informal processes within a culture that supports coaching and mentoring. Among the last network, that of professional providers, Illich describes the 'pedagogical counsellor' who provides on a personal basis the advice and guidance essential for every learner to make full use of the networks, in which:

> ... the educational path of each student would be his own to follow, and only in retrospect would it take on features of a recognizable program. The wise student would periodically seek professional advice: assistance to set a new goal, insight into difficulties encountered, choice between possible methods.

Twenty years later these ideas were re-worked by Howard Gardner, who, like Illich, was sceptical of the power of the existing education system to provide all learners with the level and quality of education now becoming essential. He similarly suggested a new set of roles for educators. First comes the 'assessment specialist' who diagnoses learner abilities and interests. Then comes the 'student-curriculum broker' who helps to match the student to particular curricula and learning styles. There follows the 'school-community broker' who matches the learner to the appropriate learning opportunities available within the community, with a particular emphasis on those opportunities rich in potential for apprenticeships, mentorships and internships. Finally, there is room for 'professional teachers' who would teach but also play a key role and giving the system overall coherence. The necessary technological and human resources essential for such a system already exist, insisted Gardner. Achieving it was a matter of will. It still is.

It is here that we must move beyond some of the traditional issues – curriculum, assessment, pedagogy, and advice and guidance – by which education systems are judged. There are now deep changes taking place very rapidly in our society and these introduce new and difficult questions about schools and schooling and about the nature of the foundations of lifelong learning. The first of these has just emerged in the argument: the new technologies. Do they make a difference?

SIX

Information, communication and learning technologies

The old computing was about what computers could do; the new computing is about what users can do. Successful technologies are those that are in harmony with users' needs. They must support relationships and activities that enrich the users' experiences. (Ben Shneiderman)

If, as experts predict, some two billion users will be on the Internet by 2005, using computer-driven feedback loops to communicate and transact virtually every mode of human enterprise, fundamental categories of community, of participatory politics, of the exchange and codification of knowledge and desire will have altered. The analogy will not be one of expected and gradual and adaptive change, but of mutation. (George Steiner)

Information and communication technology (ICT) skills have become one of the educational 'basics' alongside literacy and numeracy, and they cannot be 'dropped' as a subject on the school curriculum before the age of 16. Beyond 16, ICT remains one of the key skills in which all students ought to achieve at least a level 2 qualification, that is, equivalent to a higher grade in GCSE. In further education colleges, ICT is usually called ILT – information and learning technologies. Since in education both the information and communication aspects of the new technologies relate to learning, it seems sensible to combine the terms as ICLT – information, communication and learning technologies (ICLTs).

When ICLT skills eventually become embedded in the classroom practices of all teachers, they may be taught entirely through other subjects, but for the moment ICLT will continue also to be a separate subject taught by specialist teachers. Curriculum content achieves the status as a 'basic' when it meets two criteria: when that knowledge and skill is seen as a prerequisite for access to, and mastery of, the rest of the curriculum; and when it is thought to be knowledge and skill that will continue to be drawn on for the rest of one's life, including in the workplace.

Thus, on joining the select company of 'the basics', ICLT knowledge and skill have established their credentials as an inherent component of lifelong learning, now firmly rooted in school years. Since ministers have, from 1997, constantly proclaimed the potential of the ICLTs to exert a transformative effect on education, and have been willing to spend huge sums of money on ICLT in schools and colleges, then surely here is one aspect of government policy where both the rhetoric and the investment have secured the place of ICLT in education as one of the foundations of lifelong learning. All, apparently, is going well. Or is it?

The ICLT revolution – the rapid development of the new technology in terms of PCs, games, the Internet, e-mailing, mobiles, texting, personal digital assistants (PDAs), digital video – caught the education system largely unprepared. Schools and the teaching profession are relatively slow to change, and very few teachers were among the 'early adopters' of the new technologies. Many pupils soon became more comfortable with, or even enthusiastic users of, the ICLTs than teachers – a second kind of digital divide – and schools could not afford to buy the necessary hardware to meet what some teachers slowly began to see as both a new need and a potential opportunity. Other teachers, particularly from an older generation, having experienced the short-lived fads of teaching machines and language laboratories, defended their caution, which rationalised their defensive fear. It is never easy for the profession to accept that there is a part of the curriculum where the student is more knowledgeable and adept than the teacher.

The natural first step for the incoming New Labour government in 1997 was to invest in ICLT infrastructure – hardware and connectivity. This was very expensive indeed (to the tune of around £1.8 billion), but nobody denied that this was a necessary early step. There tended to be an implicit assumption that once the basic infrastructure was in place – broadband would have to come on stream a little later – the teachers would be equipped to usher in the ICLT revolution in education and begin the much-heralded process of transformation.

Most teachers proved to be neither ready nor willing. When the transformation did not appear, irritated policy makers asked in frustration why, when provided with all the tools, the teachers did not get on with the job. So additional New Opportunities Fund (NOF) money was found to support schemes to endow teachers with the requisite ICLT skills. These were of mixed quality; some were so poorly designed that the impact on teachers was negative. More importantly, too much attention was given to training teachers in basic ICLT skills, with little recognition that this might do very little to help them apply such skills to improve their classroom pedagogy. It is one thing to help teachers to use a computer; it is quite another to show them how to deploy those skills so that they can teach their subject more effectively and efficiently.

At this point, teachers were also under pressure to meet the DfES targets for better student performance in key stage national tests and in GCSEs. Would the ICLTs help in this regard? Did the ICLT courses that teachers followed give them a new and powerful tool to improve student test performance? Almost certainly not, in most cases. Most teachers perceived themselves to be at first base in ICLT. Yes, they had the basic skills, but many were beginners still lacking in ICLT confidence. Three things were needed if teachers were to develop the pedagogic knowledge and skill to apply the ICLTs in their lessons:

- the confidence to experiment with the ICLTs to improve their teaching, so that they could do some traditional things better;
- the space in which to experiment so that they could use the ICLTs to do some quite new things that would complement or replace traditional practices;
- the active support in all this from head teachers and senior staff.

In other words, most teachers needed considerable support if they were to engage in the innovation that would change their pedagogy. In fact, for most teachers all three conditions were lacking and, I suspect, it was only in a minority of exceptional schools that all three conditions were met.

Some of this damage, which considerably slowed up progress and failed to build on the provision of infrastructure, is being repaired. For example, the School Leadership for ICT (SLICT) courses devised by the National College for School Leadership and the British Educational and Communication Technology Agency (BECTA) are now helping head teachers to provide the kind of leadership that has long been known to be essential to the successful implementation of innovation. But the inhibitors of experimentation remain largely in place and the pressures to achieve better test and examination results are mostly intact. Most worrying of all, ministers wanted hard evidence that the ICLT investment would soon pay dividends in terms of improved student test performance, despite the fact that there were few sound reasons for believing that the schools were well placed to ensure that the ICLTs in schools would, at this very early stage when the investment in the preparation of the teachers was hugely outweighed by the scale of investment in the infrastructure, show a measurable difference in narrow achievement tests. Happily there were some indications of positive evidence for this, not surprisingly mainly in schools where the policies for ICLT had been well thought out and implemented. The danger, however, remains that the principal criterion for the success of the ICLT strategy in schools should be improved test scores.

From the lifelong learning perspective, this is a grave mistake. If this criterion continues to be applied, it will, like the policies on assessment, distort what teachers and students do and undermine the better learning and teaching that the policy was originally designed to promote. The criteria by which ICLT in schools and teachers should be judged are, from the lifelong learning perspective, their capacity to:

- improve students' learning;
- help students to learn how to learn;
- enhance students' motivation to learn.

The three criteria are interdependent. To take one alone, independently of the others, is dangerous. It is precisely because the government has focused on the first criterion, and used a very narrow measure of learning outcomes, that the policy is not working as it should. It would make more sense to start with the last criterion, since it is difficult to meet the first two criteria if the third one fails to be met.

That the new technologies are motivating to young people is self-evident. Not only are youngsters the biggest consumers of them, they also embrace them with a confident playfulness that eschews the reading of instructions and manuals – which are for the more nervous and tentative adult users – and leap quickly into active exploration of what the technology can do. Their attitude to the ICLTs is simply described: what, ask the young, can these technologies do for me? Will they help me to do things I enjoy? Games. Will they help me communicate with my mates? Mobiles. Will they help me with my homework? The Internet. Their learning is goal-driven but playful and exploratory. If the ICLTs help young people reach their goals, they will learn how to use them to best effect.

The educational challenge is that much of what students are supposed to be learning in school is not what they want to learn and is not part of their everyday life goals. But for the majority, school and its demands are accepted and they are motivated to respond positively. So if the ICLTs do help pupils get through the homework, they will be used. We should accept this instrumentalism.

One important power of the ICLTs is to generate motivation in areas of learning where, in the absence of the ICLTs, motivation would be very much lower. The ICLTs *add* motivation to the learning they accompany. They do this in a variety of ways. They may make the work *easier*. Redrafting an essay is much easier to do with computer-based text than with written text, where the whole piece has to be rewritten, slowly and painfully. The Internet or the use of some commercial software can make the task of finding relevant material to support or illustrate an argument much more efficient than searching through books. They also often make the work *more interesting*. They give speedy access to material that is often of inherent interest: in the exploration of new sources one stumbles across the unusual and fascinating.

We should not play down the motivational power of the ICLTs, even though measures of this have yet to be properly devised and then used as a criterion of ICLT effectiveness. This motivational capacity is vastly under-exploited at present, mainly because we have yet to design more educational materials with a game-like format. Computer games are attractive, but the river of investment and ingenuity that flows into commercial sector games is rarely diverted into education sector software, although the situation is improving. There is a long way to go before we solve the problem of content – online material that is appropriate for school classrooms and is presented for students in attractive and usable formats.

One can then move to the criteria more directly concerned with students' learning. Do the ICLTs make a contribution to helping students to learn how to learn? Indeed, they do, and this potential contribution, currently weak and neglected, could take three major forms. First, it has a role to play in *assessment for learning* as described in previous chapters. In particular, the ICLTs are powerful providers of formative feedback on the success with which students learn. The advantage of computer-generated feedback is that it is impersonal and so unthreatening. As a simple example, a student engaged in a piece of free writing has the text automatically spell-checked, so spelling errors can be pointed out as they are made. The correct spelling can then be suggested – as in most commercially provided spell-checks – or a program can be devised to invite the learner to attempt a correct spelling, rewarding success with praise and supplying the correct spelling if student attempts at self-correction are unsuccessful. Second, the ICLTs are powerful means of developing *investigational and research skills*, which are among the set of generic skills that comprise 'learning to learn'. Third, the ICLTs have the capacity for students to *take more responsibility for their own learning*. Most students between the ages of 11 and 16 make little progress in this regard and the debate about the teacher's role is too often polarised between a conservative emphasis on whole-class teaching, which can so easily reduce to boring lectures, and a radical espousal of more student-centred approaches, which can easily reduce to the tedium of worksheets and distraction from work as the teacher is absorbed in talk with individual students in another part of the classroom. In my view, helping students learn to take more responsibility for their learning is perhaps the most significant potential contribution of the ICLTs to establishing sound foundations for lifelong learning, but we know too little about how to achieve it. To improve our knowledge here, we need to get beyond stereotypes of 'traditional' and 'progressive' teaching to explore the new ways of organising schools and classrooms in which ICLTs will find a more natural home.

None of this will arise without teacher intervention and help. It is very easy to let students waste time surfing the Internet in search of some relevant material, ideas, evidence or illustration. Most students will need help in learning the skills of locating the right material in efficient ways, just as most students need, and in universities receive, some help in the best use of conventional libraries. Of particular importance here is helping students to learn how to *evaluate* the materials they find, for their quality and trustworthiness. Today's students need to retain less factual information in their heads than did their forbears; but they need much greater skill in knowing how to locate, identify and evaluate the information that they will need.

These skills are not acquired quickly or easily by teachers or students. In the short term, teachers who feel under pressure to incorporate ICLT in their lessons may do so in ways that are of little value. In recent times the *Daily Telegraph* has run a series of articles criticising the use of ICLT in schools; indeed, it looks rather like a campaign against ICLT in schools and claims that the investment in the infrastructure is a waste of public resources. Poor use of ICLT in classrooms is cited as an implicit attack on traditional classroom techniques such as note-taking. In one report, a student is quoted as saying:

"The Internet can be quite good but anyone can put anything on there so you should not necessarily believe it. I learn most from listening to people talk and writing down what they say."

Internet material is rightly approached with a cautious scepticism. Face-to-face talk is treated wrongly with unquestioning respect. Using computers in classrooms can amount to purposeless busy-work – so-called edutainment – in the hands of teachers without the necessary confidence and skill: that this happens is a real demonstration that the professional development of teachers lags behind the provision of hardware and software.

Denouncing bad practice in classrooms highlights the risk when politicians make exaggerated claims for the potential power of the ICLTs to improve learning in the short term. The best-documented indictment here is that by the American educationist Larry Cuban, in *Oversold and underused: Computers in the classroom* (2001). He is particularly sceptical about the rhetoric that computers in classrooms can *transform* the quality of teaching and learning, and his empirical studies, although small-scale and somewhat anecdotal, tell an important story. Cuban did find some outstanding teachers, who were able to do what is currently recognised in England as the key, namely embed ICLT in the pedagogy, or in other words, integrate ICLT into their daily routines in the classroom in a way that enriched the quality of teaching and of learning. Most teachers he watched found this difficult – and this would probably also be the case in British schools. He also found a lack of technical support: teachers too often lacked technical expertise and if machines went wrong, they could not be put right quickly and this discouraged teachers from using them at all. (Head teachers in England who invest heavily in IT technician support never regret it.)

More important, perhaps, Cuban found that few teachers were able to use the ICLTs in a way that would justify the term *transformation*, that is, introduce new practices that made significant changes in how they taught or how students learned. Most teachers displayed the uncertainty and ambivalence towards the ICLTs, leading to the very limited use, that is found in many schools in England: how many of us have visited schools and passed by empty suites of computers only to be told by a head teacher host that we have dropped in on the 'wrong' day. A high-tech school with low-tech teaching and learning! Cuban found that many teachers made minor changes to their professional practices as a result of the infusion of computers into their schools, but observed that:

> ... these small adjustments are not what the promoters of computers had in mind. They wanted to transform teaching from the familiar teacher-centred approach to one that required the teacher to play a considerably different role. Using the technology, the teacher would organise the classroom differently, giving students far more control over their learning (for example working in teams or projects) ... the teachers we interviewed and observed,

however, engaged mostly in incremental changes. Only a tiny band of teachers moved toward deeper, major reform.

As we saw in Chapter Four, the well-designed project does indeed require a very different approach to teaching and learning, but offers to achieve more in terms of both student learning *and* an enhanced capacity to learn. The present constraints on teachers in both curriculum and assessment make the use of projects a high-risk venture. The traditional timetable of short lessons also militates against the use of the ICLTs. It is a moot point whether we should create ICLT-rich schools and see if they can generate new structures and cultures in which transformed methods of teaching and learning will flourish, or whether it would be more prudent simply to encourage new ways of organising schools and see if they naturally become ICLT-rich. I incline to the latter. ICLTs have a huge contribution to make to the development of the project-based approach to learning and, as argued earlier, the present way in which schools are organised is inimical to the project. Innovative forms of school organisation are probably essential to getting the right combination of imaginative project work and highly effective use of ICLTs.

It is tempting for the ICLT enthusiasts – and for equally enthusiastic ministers and policy makers – to write off these critiques, whether they come from respected educationists or the *Daily Telegraph*, as a temporary phenomenon or as the expression of a Luddite tendency. We should never assume that the ICLTs, which cover a huge and expanding range of hardware and software, always exert a beneficial effect in education. Every use of ICLT should be subject to rigorous scrutiny to assess its impact, and particularly to see if it improves teaching and learning and, just as importantly, is worth the effort and the expenditure. Enthusiasts and detractors will be able to defend their arguments for as long as hard evidence is, as now, very hard to come by. The ICLTs should always justify their place in education by their demonstrable added value, and in the longer term not just the short-term meeting of targets for student achievement in tests. In this regard, it may be that it is particular *combinations* of ICLTs, not just single ones such as interactive whiteboards or computer suites with a weekly lesson, that make the demonstrable difference.

In the short term, however, we know that some schools and some teachers already make good use of the ICLTs, and what they do so well should be spread to other schools and teachers. The problem, in other words, is 'the dissemination of good practice'. Much more needs to be done to identify exemplary heads with whole-school ICLT policies, exemplary subject specialists who know how to integrate the ICLTs with pedagogic knowledge and skill of teaching their subject, and other forms of leading-edge innovation in the ways that the ICLTs can be used to improve education. This also means recognising that some of the most interesting innovations for disengaged young people and 'dropouts' occupy the margins, so the lessons they carry for mainstream provision are not easy to learn. The ICLTs are now paving the way to better and easier communication and interaction between the many networks of schools and teachers that are springing up. The ICLTs open the way to the *lateral* transfer of knowledge between practitioners, and these are more likely to be effective than top-down initiatives from the DfES, as we shall see in Chapter Eight. Online professional learning communities among teachers are in their infancy.

Good practice in the use of ICLT does not always flow from the school to the home. Many parents, particularly younger ones, are themselves computer-literate, providing their children with equipment, with models of flexible and creative use of computers, and with lots of practice opportunities. It is easy for teachers to feel threatened by student ICLT skill, and so become reluctant to draw on what parents can offer at home and then import into the school. The ICLTs are beginning to have an impact on home–school and parent–teacher relationships. When parents have online access to what has been set for their children's homework, as well as the materials used in lessons, they can indeed create a better partnership that prevents students playing off adults against one another, a skill most seem to acquire with astonishing ease. Schools that are developing managed learning environments (MLEs) do not merely use the ICLTs to devise sophisticated systems of information management that reduce administration, but create new links with home and community. Where sixth form students have ready access to computers at home or in study centres, there is ample opportunity to explore new ways of organising classes. If students were to work independently, at home or in centres, for two days of the week, but drawing on online support from tutors where appropriate, this would not only free teachers for more small group and individual tutorials, along the lines of university teaching, thus adding to their professional satisfaction, but it would also be a sound preparation for the greater degree of independent learning that the students will experience in higher education.

As more young teachers enter the profession, they will have grown up with the ICLTs and have much greater confidence to integrate them into their teaching, experimenting in more radical ways. And they will be working with more students and students' parents with very similar experience. At this point we will see a greater student-pull than technology-push towards innovation in the application of the ICLTs to schools and classrooms. This raises deep questions for policy makers. Conventionally they make policies that the system then has to strive to implement: the policy makers are, by definition, ahead of the game. But in the case of ICLT, policy may inevitably be *behind* the game, making *de jure* what is already *de facto* in the system, legitimating and spreading what has been shown to work.

Criteria by which government and its agencies might be evaluated are not necessarily the same as those by which schools and teachers should be judged, as outlined above. Indeed, these should include the provision of:

- an appropriate infrastructure;
- appropriate educational software;

- appropriate training for the heads, teachers and staff of schools;
- advice and support on all aspects of ICLT in schools.

In broad terms, these criteria are being met by government action. The software market is developing slowly, but now includes much more provision from the public sector, such as the BBC's contribution to Curriculum Online. BECTA, together with the DfES's ICT in Schools Division and the e-learning team, as well as ICLT advisers and coordinators in LEAs, are providing a rich supply of advice and support. But just as it has been easy to see ICLT in schools as belonging to a specialist teacher and to lessons that take place in a computer suite, so at government level it is easy for ICLT to become yet another silo in the DfES so that ICLT is not integral to policies where it is relevant, but instead becomes a somewhat awkward and haphazardly applied add-on.

Here perhaps is one of the dangers of the concept of *e-learning*. Presumably this is along the line of e-commerce or e-business, which is mainly about the buying and selling of goods on the Internet. Adding e- to an activity is becoming fashionable, as in e-healthcare and e-government. But what exactly is e-learning? Officially it is defined as follows:

> If someone is learning in a way that uses information and communication technologies, they are using e-learning.... e-learning exploits interactive technologies and communication systems to improve the learning experience. It has the potential to transform the way we teach and learn across the board.... Essentially, e-learning is about improving the quality of learning through using interactive computers, on-line communications and information systems in ways that other teaching methods cannot match.

The danger is that if e-learning encourages the view that it is a distinctive type of learning, and if the sister concept of *e-teaching* becomes a distinctive method of teaching, then the idea that the ICLTs should be integrated or 'embedded' in the everyday teaching and learning in schools may be damaged, since after successful integration the ICLTs become a natural element in what happens when people teach or learn. The concepts of e-learning and e-teaching may unintentionally make it less likely that less confident teachers will embrace the possibilities offered to them by the ICLTs. Teachers draw on different tools in their teaching, and students draw on a range of tools in their learning, according to their fitness for purpose. ICLTs add to the range of tools and should be regarded by every teacher and every learner as a wonderful set of extra resources – just as books and writing materials have been treated in the past. We must take care that the rhetoric of the ICLT revolution does not lead to the bursting of an e-learning bubble.

If the ICLTs are used sensibly, profitably and naturally by learners during their school years, under the influence of teachers who also use them in the same way, it will be easier for learners in their later lives to access educational provision that is heavily imbued with the new technologies, such as Learndirect or The Open University and, increasingly, many other forms of further, adult and community education, as well as work-based learning opportunities that are part of life's learning journey. Most important of all, through their use of the ICLTs that pervade life in the home, they will help to fuse education and leisure. In homes where reading is a source of pleasure for adults, the intrinsic motivation to read among the young is greater. ICLTs will go the same way. Learning as pleasure is at the heart of lifelong learning.

As George Steiner (2003) has said of the new technologies:

> Computation, information theory and retrieval, the ubiquity of the Internet and the global web enact far more than a technological revolution. They entail transformations of awareness, of habits of perception and articulation, of reciprocal sensibility which we are scarcely beginning to gauge.... The impact on the learning process is already momentous.... Conditions of collaborative exchange and debate, of memory storage, of immediate transmission and graphic representation have already reorganized numerous aspects of *Wissenschaft*. The screen can teach, examine, demonstrate, interact with a precision, a clarity, and a patience exceeding that of a human instructor.... Its resources can be disseminated and enlisted at will. It knows neither prejudice nor fatigue.

If so, what are the implications of this for schools, the basic design of which originated in a different age?

SEVEN

School design

There is no doubt whatever about the influence of architecture and structure upon human character and action. We shape our buildings, and afterwards our buildings shape us. (Winston S. Churchill)

If you want to study learning, the last place to look is in the school. (Jean Lave)

School buildings have, over the last 20 years or more, been badly neglected. It has been easy to divert scarce resources to other priorities – leaking roofs, planned repainting and refurbishment, new buildings and so on – as these can always be postponed for another year or two. Eventually, as now, however, these matters can no longer be deferred. The question is, will the opportunity created by the massive, multi-billion pounds building programme over the next few years be used to redesign schools for the future? If lifelong learning means access to learning opportunities for everyone, anytime, anywhere, does this not entail a radical reappraisal of the school and the way it is designed? Or will, as so often in the past, architects design schools in line with their own sad stereotypes of what a school should look like, with little reference to those who use schools?

The outlook is brighter than it has been. At all levels, including officials in the DfES, there are people who are determined not to let this unique opportunity slip away. David Miliband, the minister for school standards, has established a 'Building Schools for the Future' programme by which 12 exemplar designs, six primary and six secondary, are being commissioned. The problem is that there remains uncertainty and disagreement about what exactly schools of the 21st century are for. As in the case of churches, there is widespread agreement that traditional designs have shortcomings, but also confusion over fresh designs that might set things right. Few would disagree that school designs ought to be adapted to fit the concept of lifelong learning, and thus of more efficient usage by more people, since too many schools are underused in the evenings, at weekends and during holidays. Yet this acknowledgement provides neither much practical guidance on the kinds of change that should be made, nor any guarantee that a very different kind of building will ensure better usage.

There are four main constraints against making radical changes to site design. The first derives from the neglect of school buildings and the shameful state into which many premises have fallen. In these circumstances, many teachers simply want a school in which the roof does not leak, the walls are freshly painted, rooms are reasonably furnished and the chairs (including those in the staff room) are comfortable. Such modest aspirations tend to occlude ambitions for a fundamental redesign.

The second and related constraint is a widespread and deeply conservative attitude to the school as an institution. Schools have traditionally been designed to consist mainly of classrooms shaped to hold some 20 to 30 desks or tables for students and a larger desk/table for the teacher, with a blackboard or whiteboard at the 'front'. In addition, rather different spaces are needed for 'practical' subjects such as science, technology, art, home economics and so on. Larger spaces are required for a gymnasium/sports centre, for a library, and for an assembly, conventionally designed to hold all the students for religious and other purposes, including public performances, such as events in drama and music. While many doubt whether the traditional school hall can be justified – it is empty for much of the time – it is far from clear whether traditional classrooms should now occupy the majority of the space, and if not, what might replace them. There is, however, general agreement that any design needs to be highly *flexible*, in part because the way space is used is likely to change over time; and in part because many spaces must be open to use by different groups of people for different purposes at different times.

While many teachers are prepared to be at least open-minded on the matter of school design, many parents are deeply conservative. They view schools with nostalgia through the rose-tinted lenses of their own schooldays, and they want schools to be safe and secure places for their children. Their natural inclination is therefore to opt for the familiar. As a result, schools become distinctive entities that are separated from the rest of life. In small villages the football and cricket teams play on fields that are not the primary school's grounds; the players shower in pavilions – used just once a week – rather than in the school's facilities. In many villages adults spend years raising funds for a village hall, with little thought about sharing some space with the local school – and this, ironically, in Cambridgeshire, the home of Henry Morris' pioneering village colleges that changed conceptions of community education. Nor is this merely a rural phenomenon. When I worked in inner London, adult education centres were often part of a secondary school building, but the two were treated in practice as if they were totally separate entities, located miles apart. In many places, especially in areas of deprivation, community centres are attached to public libraries rather than schools. Part of the problem is that adult spaces need and can tolerate largely open access, whereas nowadays schools have to be very much on their guard against intruders and prowlers, and parents rightly expect this.

Consequently schools are often disassociated and disconnected from adult leisure and learning. Schools are for children: adults have their own facilities. Those places where these crude stereotypes have been shattered through radical versions of community education and shared facilities remain a minority and their ideas have been very slow to spread. Pioneering designs, such as the

Sutton Centre in Nottingham, have been far less influential than one might have assumed.

In most localities achieving a broad-based coalition of interests among disparate groups, many of whom like their own distinctive space, on the design of schools of the future will be difficult to achieve. Doubtless part of the problem is the very word *school*. Perhaps change would be easier to manage if we could get rid of this word and replace it with some new term. But what might this be? Obvious candidates, such as *neighbourhood learning centre*, are not always appropriate, since schools may not actually serve a neighbourhood or even a specific locality. Yet it would make sense to combine schools with health centres and begin to integrate local services for children, as has happened in Hertfordshire. In the light of the Green Paper, *Every child matters*, it is likely that the various agencies and services for children and families will be much better coordinated and perhaps integrated. Here is another constraint, the difficulty of ensuring 'joined-up government' at national or local level. It is exceptionally difficult to join up the different segments of the DfES: it is divided into silos, and despite much readiness of senior officials, lateral coordination proves to be highly elusive. Getting two or more departments at national level, for example, Health and Education, to work together or to coordinate funding is yet more difficult, and interdepartmental collaboration at local level is often equally resistant to coordination. The spirit behind *Every child matters* is admirable, but experience of past reforms does not inspire confidence that much will be achieved.

This is unfortunate, since a more coherent approach by the many agencies and services to children and families might lead to radical rethinking about what happens in school, and therefore about the design of the premises in which these services are provided. It has long been known that where parents take an interest in their children's education, where they actively support it, and are prepared to do so in the home, for example by listening to their children read, then the children are more successful and happy in school. Closing the gap in achievement and attitude between the higher and lower socioeconomic groups – and thus laying better and more equitable foundations for lifelong learning – unquestionably means finding ways of helping parents in the lower socioeconomic groups to play a more active and positive role in their children's education. It is often these very parents who had a poor experience of school during their own childhood and for whom the concept, image and actual buildings of the school remain negative and alien. Redesigning school buildings in the light of more coherent services for children and families is thus an opportunity we cannot afford to miss.

For some, all this means is that the school should disappear and be replaced by the *neighbourhood learning centre*. But many schools no longer serve the local community living close by. Instead, parental choice has in many places hastened the demise of the neighbourhood comprehensive school. In any event it has been shown that schools adopt very different models to the community, either as a geographical entity or as the body of the pupils' parents. Some schools want to share their resources with the community and welcome adults into the school for a variety of activities. Others shun the parents and see their duty as maximising the achievement of students who have been entrusted to the care of the school. Moreover these different approaches to relations with the community often reflect the philosophy of the head teacher, and when the head changes, so too does the model of community relations.

Perhaps it is the *primary* school that should be the community centre, but even here parental choice has extended the catchment area far beyond the immediate locality (in the village where I live, half the children in the primary school come from outside the village). Moreover, it is secondary schools, with their sports halls and other facilities, that are attractive and amenable to parent and adult use, rather than primary schools, with their tiny chairs.

The best hope may lie in the recent development of collegiates and federations, where groups of schools develop stronger links of many different kinds and with variable degrees of integration. Such a group of schools can offer parental choice but nevertheless see themselves as having a shared commitment not to a local community but to a common *area*. Since collegiates/federations may in any event share facilities and offer complementary resources to one another and to their community area, significant questions arise about how the buildings and facilities of a collegiate or federation might be designed. This could be the greatest hope for some radical rethinking that could exert a profound influence on conceptions of lifelong learning for coming generations.

The final constraint is the internal administration of schools, which are conventionally divided into age cohorts of year-groups, and each of these sub-divided into classes, the unit that occupies a classroom. There are exceptions, such as vertically grouped classes of pupils of mixed ages in primary schools, but they are treated as outside the norm. It is usually held that this form of organisation is the best in which to help children to learn.

The truth is that schools are organised in this way because it is, quite simply, the most administratively convenient – for the teachers, of course – way of organising life in school that has yet been invented. Year-groups are convenient because the curriculum is designed around the school year, beginning in the autumn and ending in the summer, after which that age cohort 'moves up' into the next year-group, often with a new teacher or teachers. Admission to the school can often be restricted to the beginning of a year or a term. Placing children born in the same year, arbitrarily beginning in September of the new school year, in the same class has disadvantages, especially for the summer-born children who will be almost a year younger than the rest of their peers with whom they will spend the rest of their school years – this is a troubling fact that is simply ignored. Despite much rhetoric to the contrary, pupils are difficult to treat as individuals: as year-groups and classes they can be controlled as collectivities, making life for the staff very much easier.

The year-group structure of schools is very rarely questioned. It may have been of little consequence when most children left school for work by the age of 12. But as the school leaving age has risen to 16, and as even that age has ceased to be the point at which the majority end their participation in formal education and training, the effect of year-grouping has been the single most important factor in the creation of a teenage culture since the 1950s. Once established through schooling, the adolescent society has been reinforced by an active commercial market that exploits to the full their isolation from the rest of society, which from the adolescents' point of view is neatly divided into two alien parts: children and adults. Of all the societies that have existed in the history of the human race, it is industrialised nations – for the modern school was the invention of the industrial revolution – that have placed teenagers in this strange no-man's land of being no longer a child and not yet an adult. Not surprisingly, adolescence is a more troublesome stage of life in our kind of society than it has ever been in the past. The principal source of this social segregation of teenagers is the school, and its distinctive social organisation into year-groups for the administrative convenience of the teaching profession. Today, we easily treat the phenomenon as entirely natural and so as unquestionable.

One of the most striking consequences of age cohorts based on school year-grouping has been the introduction of psychological boundaries not merely between different year-groups but more powerfully between adults and adolescents. For members of one side to spend too much time with the other is to breach the boundary and invoke the sanctions of curiosity and disapproval. Many adults feel uneasy in the company of a group of young people outside their family – feelings that are reciprocated by many young people. This explains why teachers are not perceived by many students to be 'real' people at all. In the role of teacher-in-school they have a special status that, in a curious parallel to the ambiguity of adolescent status, makes them not-yet-a-normal-adult but also not-really-one-of-us. Thus it is that many students experience an awkward embarrassment when they meet their teacher in a non-school environment, such as the supermarket.

It is these factors that hinder the greater involvement of adults in schools. Most adults and most young people are simply not really at ease in one another's presence, especially if the occasion is one in which both might be learning. This is deeply tragic, for there have been a number of experiments over recent years to introduce adults into secondary school classrooms, where the presence of these AoTs (or adults other than teachers) has had a salutary effect on the behaviour and work habits of many young people, especially those who are disengaged, where the adults play the role of *mentors* as well as fellow learners. It has to be admitted, however, that some teachers remain uncomfortable with AoTs in their classrooms. Teachers form idiosyncratic relationships with their adolescent charges that bear observation only from sympathetic fellow teachers. Teachers, adults and children seem to be able to be at ease with one another only during the early years of primary education: with each successive year the sense of discomfort rises, the pressure to part company increases, and the ideal of young people, teachers and adults learning together in a formal setting steadily recedes.

But that might change if schoolwork was organised around the *project* as defined earlier, rather than the lesson-in-the-classroom – the project being an activity in which students and adults can be together far more naturally than in the classroom. The students, and their adult *mentors*, need real problems to solve and/or a real end product or service to produce. There has to be a genuine challenge that requires them to act responsibly and to make decisions that have consequences for themselves and others. There has to be a demand to learn something – acquire new knowledge or a new skill – to solve the problem and develop a product – and that need has to be generated by the task, and not the teacher. They must have space in which to work independently and in a 'hands-on' way, which makes ready access to the new technologies essential. Opportunities to make mistakes and to learn from them are essential. There has to be an occasion to celebrate success and to make it known to significant others. And as much of this as possible should take place away from conventional school premises.

Such a change would take many years to implement, and in the shorter term there is a real need to meet the needs of disengaged youngsters. For them the challenge is quite simply to take the schooling out of school as much as possible, especially during their adolescent years, and to relocate learning in a context in which lifelong learning is more at home.

A useful starting premise is that many young people, especially – but by no means exclusively – those who are disaffected and who turn against formal education and lifelong learning despite having the greatest need for it, simply outgrow school. Previous generations put up with school. Their equivalents today are more likely to walk out of school: the current high rates of absenteeism have proved to be very stubborn, even against imaginative and expensive schemes to reduce them. If those who 'bunk off' stay in, or are returned to, school, they tend to be openly rebellious and disruptive of those students, often a majority, who fall within the spectrum of liking school or being willing to put up with it. Policy makers are inclined to invent measures to reduce disaffection or to segregate disruptive students from mainstream provision. Public opinion is barely satisfied by these manoeuvres: the populist solution would be to 'get tough' on deviants and return to a more traditional and harsher school discipline, combined with threats to fine or jail uncooperative parents. Another suggested remedy is that the miscreants be allowed to leave school – in effect, reduce the school leaving age. This is, I think, closer to the mark, for it at least recognises that school is part of the problem and that these young people often behave very much better in the different situation of the workplace.

This solution did work once, when there was a place in many parts of industry and business for unskilled workers who needed to be barely, if at all, literate and numerate, but this is no longer the case. Business and industry do not want such 14- and 15-year-olds. They may take young people if there were some kind of guarantee that they would arrive with a good grasp of the basics and also had the *generic skills* discussed earlier – being punctual and reliable, able to manage themselves and solve problems without close supervision, communicating well and working effectively in a team. But most of the young people who leave school early do not have this set of skills. To most business and industries, they would therefore be a liability. Freeing them from formal education would be to abandon them to unemployment at a vulnerable age and it is well known what fate awaits such people in later years.

The answer must lie in a variety of 'half-way houses' between full-time school and full-time work. For some this could be entry to an apprenticeship, half-time in occupation and half-time in education – although probably a college of further education rather than a school – with the curriculum closely focused on the needs of work-related knowledge and skill. Discovering that learning helps you to enjoy and be successful at work is often the first positive step on the path to lifelong learning. This cannot, however, be the solution for all. We are already asking much of employers and there are limits to what they, and especially small and medium-sized enterprises (SMEs), can offer to solve the problem. The education service has to engage in internal reform rather than imagining that employers can do it alone.

Lifelong learning, often in the form of continuing professional development, is flourishing in many workplaces. A huge investment is taking place in both the private and public sectors for building educational opportunities into the working environment and into career structures. This is leading to some redesign of the workplace, as well as to changing attitudes to on-the-job learning and to developing the skills of mentoring and coaching. There may not be much room to place large numbers of young people in the workplace, but there is some room. More importantly, we need to devise means by which the attitudes and practices of the modern workplace, and perhaps some of the staff, could be deployed on the half-way house projects that lie between school and work.

The more that young people at-risk have opportunities to experience such a half-way world at an early point on the path to disengagement, the better the chance that they can be reintegrated into some form of education and training, whatever form it takes and wherever it takes place. Schools and classrooms get defined as *learning spaces*, when the requirement of lifelong learning is that we need *spaces for learning,* and these can be in the home, the workplace or the leisure centre, for example: any space can be transformed into a space for learning as and when it is appropriate to do so. And the more that teachers themselves begin to participate in half-way house projects, the more time they spend outside the learning space we call a school or a classroom, the more they convert very different locations into spaces for learning, then the more such learning will leak back into schools. It is from such experience that the vision and the will for more sustained and fruitful approaches to the redesign of schools will arise – redesigning schools follows, rather than precedes, rethinking education.

This is the time to engage in serious longer-term thinking about how a school that makes the *project* its central organisational principle for learning might need to be designed. And if a collegiate or federation of schools were to adopt the *project* as a fundamental unit of learning and teaching, then radical redesign of the school would be patently essential. In my view, it is in the combination of *project* methodology in a collegiate or federation of schools that involves a wide range of AoTs from their collective community area as *mentors* that my hope for new designs to support lifelong learning resides. For it is extremely unlikely that we can advance lifelong learning by minor tampering with the design of the school. And even were a far-sighted head teacher to achieve a fundamental redesign, there is no guarantee that this would change what happens thereafter. One of the lessons to be learnt from the modest redesign for open-plan primary schools is that many teachers quickly moved cupboards and bookcases, transforming them into partitions that recreated the former classroom structure. Radical redesign can leave conservative teaching practices entirely undisturbed. Unless, teachers will argue, we are convinced of the need to reconsider the nature of teaching and learning for young people, why should we take an interest in the redesign of schools? Until very recently, teachers have not been accustomed to thinking of schools as *their* premises, but rather as belonging to the LEA, against which they feel relatively powerless. Those who favour radical redesign in the interest of lifelong learning have many deep-seated preconceptions to overcome among their potential allies.

Conventional teachers are not trained to take the kinds of role now being outlined for them. Because they grew up and prospered in the school in which for the most part they were happy and successful, as soon as they enter initial teacher training they are instantly at home and comfortable with the organisation of the school in year-groups and the structure of the day into lessons for classes. They do not need persuading that this is administratively convenient: they know it intuitively because the world of the school is in their bones. When, in due course, they witness the resistance to school from many adolescents, they are disinclined to seek a radical solution. And if the radical solution were to be introduced, they are not well prepared to lead it. This has huge implications for the nature of the profession, as we shall examine in Chapter Nine.

Are we making any progress in moving toward such a solution? Yes, and in several ways: some of the seeds are to be found within the school and some within the world of work. Within the school, there is an increasing challenge to the tradition that at school level the system is strongly producer-led. In other words, in our present system it is largely a matter for the teachers to decide what the school has to offer students as well as the form in which that offer will be delivered to them. There is very little sense of the consumers, whether they be students or their parents, determining the offer or its delivery. It is sometimes said that a key reform of recent years, under both Conservative and New Labour governments, has been the extension of *choice* to the school's consumers and the construction of a market for them, and that specialist schools are an extension of choice. This argument can be misleading. While it is true that many (but not all) get a choice of school, there is relatively little in terms of customisation *within* the school. It is in this area that radical reform is needed.

It was said in the early days of the Ford motor company that you could have a car of any colour you wanted – so long as it was black. By the end of the 20th century the Japanese car industry simply asked its customers what kind of car they wanted and then customised it to meet the stated requirements. It was a revolution that forced the American automobile industry on the defensive. Which of the two approaches does our school system most resemble? I would argue that it is the early Ford approach, in which the student may choose a school but then has to conform to the standard way its services are offered. This is unlike what is happening in most private services. People are able to choose between shops or travel agents, for example, and while the content of what they sell may not differ much, their capacity to customise their services is highly variable and market-sensitive. Schools, by contrast, vary very little in their internal organisation into year-groups and classes. Interestingly, what teachers do with pupils is customised in the early years, from ages four to seven, then gets much more standardised in terms of organisation and content between eight to 14; a degree of customisation resumes in key stage four, with greater curriculum choice, which is further extended after the age of 16.

In education, what is elsewhere called *customisation* is now being called *personalisation* or *personalised learning*. It is the process of shaping the school's provision around the needs, aptitudes and interests of each individual student. In the language of ministers and DfES officials, care is taken to ensure that personalised learning is not confused with, or interpreted as, a return to child-centred philosophies and practices. Rather it is linked to some fashionable ideas among teachers, such as adapting teaching style to match students' learning styles – although several researchers have thrown doubt on the validity and value of the idea of learning styles.

The term *personalised learning* has the disadvantage that, like e-learning, it can easily be misunderstood as a form of learning. *Personalisation*, although sounding like jargon, reminds us that it is a *process* that is being talked about, requiring providers (education professionals) to do things differently for their clients (parents and students).

Is it sheer coincidence that the period of least customisation, key stages two and three, is when the growth of disengagement and disaffection is at its most acute? A lesson may be that we should pay much more attention to how the school's offer can be more customised for pupils between the ages of eight and 14 – an issue that is not currently high on the policy agenda. This is the point when students are all made to follow a curriculum that is broad and balanced, so that they are given access to all the subjects and disciplines, from which they may choose after the age of 14 as they enter key stage four.

Personalisation would therefore have to be in pedagogy or organisation, rather than curriculum, as the way of meeting individual needs. Almost certainly this would entail finding ways in which student voice in this phase could be better articulated in the construction of feasible alternatives to conventional classes and lessons. Hitherto key stage three has not been a stage in which innovation has been encouraged – the RSA's *Opening minds* project is a notable exception

– yet it is here that project-type organisation and pedagogy might matter most. It is the *project* that is the key to *personalisation*, especially in key stage three, where *generic skills* can also be embedded: this is what the pioneers of new ways of constructing key stage three have discovered. Were it possible to provide such *personalisation*, it is likely to forestall many later problems among older students when negative attitudes and disruptive behaviour can become irremediable.

The process of *personalisation* assumes that those who control our education system know how to innovate and are free to do so as a way of transforming education. Do they?

EIGHT

Innovation

Too many leaders say they want innovation but behave in ways that stifle it. (Rosabeth Moss Kanter)

If we want people's intelligence and support, we must welcome them as co-creators. People only support what they create. (Margaret J. Wheatley)

Innovation, like creativity, is one of the current buzz words in education – by which I mean it is treated as a positive, even exciting, concept among teachers and has recently been taken up by education ministers and the DfES. Conventionally innovation has been defined as:

> ... the exploitation of a new idea through practical action that adds value to a product, process or service.

This immediately removes two popular misconceptions: that an innovation is simply a new idea, which is the first element in an innovation, but not the innovation itself; and secondly that an innovation must be a product or service, as is often so in industry, when innovation can just as readily be a *process*, and in particular the process of designing an organisation and its operation. The business guru Peter Drucker offered a definition of innovation as:

> ... a change that creates a new dimension of performance.

which would appeal to those who think of education as being largely concerned with the performance of teachers. I prefer, for application in education, innovation to be defined as:

> doing things differently in order to do them better,

which can mean a modest adjustment to what one has done hitherto or a much more dramatic change in that one does something new to replace previous practice. The emphasis on 'better' is important, for we cannot blindly assume that an innovation is inherently a good thing, an advance on what went before. An innovation is not necessarily more effective or efficient than current practice. An innovation can spread in educational circles because it is imposed on the profession or because it becomes the temporary fad or fashion. We ought to test whether or not an innovation really is an improvement, but the test is by no means always undertaken before an innovation is taken up. A corollary of this test is that because it is a real improvement it should displace some previous practice. Educational innovations should not be a net addition to what teachers do. For teachers *innovations* have sometimes become synonymous with centre-led, top-down *initiatives,* which have indeed often been an addition to what teachers do rather than a replacement, and this explains in part why some of them have been resisted and treated as a burden.

Innovations vary in degree. There is *incremental* innovation, which is a minor change that is close to existing practice, as against *radical* innovation, which is a major change that is far from current practice. The first tends to be a gradual or evolutionary process, whereas the second is a discontinuous or disruptive process. The mobile phone was a radical innovation that disrupted the telecommunications market; all the subsequent modifications, which include making it smaller and lighter, are incremental innovations. There are innovations of different types. In education there are, as elsewhere, technological innovations; but of particular importance are *organisational* innovations, which include how schools are structured and managed, and *methodological* innovations, which include how teachers define and execute their teaching role and how students learn – both of which were illustrated in previous chapters.

By this point it is, I think, clear to us all that the foundations of lifelong learning in schools are not going to be improved without innovation. The questions before us, therefore, are:

- What sorts of innovation are needed to establish better foundations for lifelong learning in the school sector?
- What action needs to be taken by whom to initiate and then disseminate such innovations?

The answer to the first question is only partly clear. Certainly it would involve changes of a rather deep kind, but whether this is achievable incrementally by a slow process of change over a long period, which presumably would be relatively painless for those involved in the change, or whether more radical innovation is essential, which would be painfully disruptive of current practice, is a moot point. Could, for instance, slavery have been abolished in Britain by a slow process of changing people's minds and behaviour, by a strategy of defining current 'good practice' with slaves and then attempting to disseminate it to the rest of society? Or was more radical, disruptive action, including legislation, a necessary step? Some of the reforms mooted in the last chapter seem closer to the radical than to the incremental model. Does this necessarily mean that ministers will be frightened off?

There are clear indications that government is of the view that we need a more coherent account of the nature of education and its provision in a knowledge-based economy. Put simply, this is an acceptance by education ministers that more people need to be better educated than ever before, that the ways in which people learn and where and how they do so are changing, and that this learning must continue throughout life and so learning opportunities and incentives must also be lifelong. In this sense, government subscribes to the principle of lifelong learning, even if the term itself appears relatively rarely in what they say about education. However, this understanding has led ministers to take a rather different view of the process of change, for they now talk of the *transformation* of education and schools rather than their mere *improvement*. This suggests a new political sensitivity to the scale or depth of change that is probably involved. References to their repeated championing of innovation are in line with this interpretation. Consider the following statements taken from policy documents published over the last six years:

> Across many sectors of the economy and many aspects of our lives, the pace of innovation is dramatic. New thinking about leadership and management, operational research, new uses of ICT and the ever-increasing pressure for high quality have led to a transformation in many knowledge-based industries. *Teaching and learning should not be exempt from this revolution.* It is striking that so far the teaching and learning process has stayed remarkably stable is spite of huge structural changes in the last decade or so. We believe that ... we must expect change in the nature of schooling. (DfEE, 1997; emphasis added)

> People who generate bright ideas and have the practical abilities to turn them into successful products and services are vital not just to the creative industries but to every sector of business. Our whole approach to what and how we learn from the earliest stages of learning needs to adapt and change to respond to this need. Academic achievement remains essential but it must increasingly be delivered through a rounded education which fosters creativity, enterprise and innovation.... [Such an education] to the benefit of learners and businesses depends on the very highest standards of teaching and learning and on the ability of teachers and lecturers to enhance the way young people learn so as to develop those capabilities.... We will foster creativity and enterprise across our education and training system through *radical new approaches to teaching and learning*.... (DTI and DFEE, 2001; emphasis added)

> We want to be able to encourage and respond to innovative approaches to teaching and learning and school management from across the secondary system. To make sure we can do this, we intend to establish a school innovation unit [which] will act as the powerhouse and incubator for new approaches, *which might not fit the rules as they currently exist*.... (DfES, 2001; emphasis added)

> We want schools to feel freer to take control, and to use their freedom to take a fresh look at their curriculum and *the organisation of the school day and week*.... (DfES, 2003; emphasis added)

With the mention of revolution and radical new approaches both to teaching and learning and to the organisation of the school day and week, it would appear that radical innovations of the kind that emerged in the previous chapter are on the government's educational agenda.

Ministers express surprise that so few schools apply to them for formal permission to work outside current regulations and to try different ways of providing education. Yet, in the light of the culture of compliance in the education service, aided and abetted by the OfSTED regime, it is their surprise that surprises. It reveals their lack of comprehension of how most head teachers and teachers read the government's intentions and invitations. They do not feel that they enjoy much autonomy and certainly less than the government claims they have. There is a very deep difference of perspective over how much 'real' autonomy schools and teachers have. The national curriculum and what have come to be called the three T's of *targets, tests* and (league) *tables* are claimed by practitioners to entail a severe curtailment of their freedom to manoeuvre. Moreover, they see their autonomy as closely circumscribed by the excessive accountability to multiple masters – to the government through regulation and performance measures, to OfSTED through the inspection regime, to LEAs, to school governing bodies and to parents. This heavy accountability encourages playing safe, not embarking on innovation, especially since some of the groups to whom schools are accountable tend to be conservative in their expectations of teachers.

This cautious, reactive response is confirmed by the blame culture that teachers believe holds sway. Innovation by definition means taking risks: the more radical the innovation, the greater the risk. The greatest sin is to fail: the worst that can befall one is be labelled 'a failing school'. Schools that do well by the government's criteria of success, the three T's, have little reason to innovate, despite being a school that has acquired the so-called 'earned autonomy' to do so. Ironically it is the schools at the point of failure that have little or nothing to lose by taking a high risk.

Risk is inescapable in innovation, a point emphasised by all who have led innovation in the business sector. "The fastest way to succeed is to double your failure rate", proclaims Thomas Watson the chief at IBM. "Fail often to succeed sooner", advises Tom Kelley of IDEO. And most wisely of all, "You must learn to fail intelligently", says the great Thomas Edison. "Failing is one of the greatest arts in the world. One fails forward towards success". Head teachers and teachers need to believe that they are allowed to fail in their innovations without recrimination or condemnation, provided that they take a very carefully calculated risk based on professional experience and judgement, and that if they do nevertheless fail, lessons will be learned and shared with other innovators.

There is also the matter of just how radical teachers could afford to be. Ministerial statements of the kind quoted above ostensibly encourage innovation of a deep kind that questions much that is taken for granted – accepted ways of teaching and learning, school management, the school day and year. Ministers might have implicitly in mind a much more limited view of what is radical, such as *lengthening* the school day or year, but not rethinking to the point where the school day no longer takes its traditional, recognisable form. Many teachers feel that the history of schooling and the form schools took at the time of the industrial revolution continue to be a heavy hand on their 21st-century descendants. In the first days of mass schooling, the function of schools was to socialise the rural young into the ways of urban living and in particular to prepare them for life on the factory floor. There is a direct correspondence between the two types of organisation. Thus it was that Charles Dickens in *Hard Times* could paint Mr Gradgrind in such harsh colours, driving out the spirit, creativity and the joy in learning of his charges who were being so carefully prepared for the deadening life of the factory floor.

Modern workplaces have changed, sometimes radically, and mostly for the better. But would the staff of one of today's schools dare to visit the most desirable of contemporary workplaces and then engage in some reverse engineering to help determine the organisation and operation of a schooling system that would prepare young people for life in such a work environment? Could one start with an acceptance of the power and potential of the new technologies and then design schooling around them, rather than as we do now, accept the conventional design of schools and try to fit the information, communication and learning technologies (ICLTs) into a shape which is remarkably inappropriate for them? The Open University was a brilliantly successful radical innovation precisely because it began from a very different set of initial premises than any other of the 'new' universities, which have been remarkably like the old universities and have mostly learned little. No mainstream university could have evolved in The Open University: there had to be a clean break with previous conceptions of how a university might operate. "We are at our best when we are at our boldest", says Tony Blair, but has there been anything in education policy since 1997 that has been as bold as The Open University? There might be a lesson for lifelong learning here.

This is not to deny, of course, the power of incremental innovation, the relatively slow process of improvement. But it is to assert that getting the foundations of lifelong learning right at the level of schools may require a bolder break with tradition and convention. There are potentially two ways of doing this, one that is internal to the school system and one that is external to it.

The internal approach sets up a group of volunteer schools to embark on a pathfinder project to find ways in which the foundations of lifelong learning can be secured: it would be another version of 'schools for the future' exercises that have been undertaken frequently in recent years. This could be a project under the auspices of government, along the lines of the ICT Test Beds project, in which families of schools and colleges are saturated with ICLT hardware and software to explore the potential of ICLT for innovation in teaching and learning as well as school management and administration. Alternatively, it could be managed and coordinated by a voluntary body. There is evidence of such experience in the RSA's *Opening minds* (referred to in Chapter Two) in which five schools embarked on a three-year project to teach Year 7 students a curriculum devised around competences (for learning, for citizenship, for relating to people, for managing situations, and for managing information) rather than based on separate subjects, which led to a different organisation, including more group work and more time with fewer teachers. The Campaign for Learning's 'learning to learn' project is a further example.

The schools would collectively define what the best foundations for lifelong learning would be in terms of curriculum, assessment, pedagogy, the new technologies and school organisation, and then each participating school would implement these foundations, in whole or part, depending on their particular circumstances and the values and preferences of their various stakeholders. Government would, where appropriate, suspend existing regulations and grant permission to innovate. The project would be closely monitored and any lessons being learned would be fed back into the system. The real test of the project would come many years later, the precise length depending on whether the participating schools included primary as well as secondary schools, but probably needing 10-15 years to test the impact on conventional educational outcomes, such as performance in public examinations, as well as those specifically sensitive to the goals of lifelong learning, such as motivation to learn, the skills of learning to learn, participation in formal and informal learning, and so on. Such an unusually long time-frame might suggest that the project should be initiated immediately: if we really do want to get the sort of knowledge the project might reveal, there is no time to lose. At the same time, it is difficult to judge just how radical such a project might be, since the degree of radicalism depends not so much on ministerial decision, but on the consent of governors, teachers, parents and students, many of whom might be very cautious about 'experiments' of this kind. Naturally compromises would have to be made, but there might be so many that nothing very radical could survive the negotiations.

The external approach would explore a radical option by being based completely outside the school system. There is the potential for such a project in the rights parents enjoy under the 1944 Education Act to educate their children 'otherwise', that is, otherwise than in school: for the Act wisely made *education*, not *school*, compulsory. The number of parents who withdraw their children from school to teach them at home or in some other place is small, but they have been growing steadily, both in this country and elsewhere. They take direct control of their children's education for a variety of motives. Sometimes it is to protect the child from the dangers they see in school life; sometimes it is because they believe that the child will be happier and better educated at home; sometimes it is a belief that the heart of a good education lies in getting the parent–child relationship right.

Various support systems for home education have sprung up in recent years and it is not difficult for a parent to get advice and help. But it remains a relatively unorganised movement. Here, however, are the seeds of a radical option for lifelong learning – if a group of these parents were to band together for two purposes: to make a shared design for establishing the foundations for lifelong learning; and then to pool ideas and resources to articulate and systematise their ideas and practices. There are several reasons why this might be a more successful challenge than the internal approach. The participants are not constrained by existing buildings, nor must they obtain approval or consent for what they do from others, such as DfES and LEA officials, governors, or parents of a whole school. Often they are parents who work from home for part of the week. They are therefore well-organised and familiar with the power of the new technologies, which they readily deploy to support their children's learning. They are models of good planning, showing how work and leisure intertwine in highly flexible ways. They are often adept at exploiting the education resources that are widely available in the community's public places, especially libraries and museums, and at brokering relationships with trusted adults from whom, and with whom, the young can learn. By getting together, a group of home education parents might collectively offer more radical and more constructive alternatives to conventional schools than is possible when each family is working in relative isolation from others.

Politicians would, of course, be nervous about appearing to support home education, since to do so acknowledges openly that there is something wrong with schooling, that the education service is dysfunctional for some young people. While ministers concede that 'one size does not fit all', this is a means of advocating change within the school system, for example the growth of specialist schools, rather than suggesting that there are some young people for whom *any* school is undesirable. There are severe limits to which ministers can expose the system's depth of malfunction: it is much safer politically to invent streams of new 'initiatives' and proliferate public bodies concerned with some aspect or other of education, all of which purport to solve the problems of mass schooling, than even to hint that some of these problems are quite simply insoluble within the present school system and that there are strict limits to the fruitfulness of more tinkering.

Yet the lessons from such a project may be less in the apparent promotion of home education that ministers would at all costs seek to avoid – unnecessarily in my view, since home schooling will be the preserve of a tiny minority for the foreseeable future – than in the flow of inventive ideas for truly radical changes within the school system. An external project could provide a better guide to 'schools of the future' than projects that focus directly on such schemes. I suspect in any event there will in future years be bridges built between the home-schoolers and mainstream provision, for instance by the use of part-time schooling. It is surely odd that after the age of 16 we accept a mixture of part-time work and part-time formal education as perfectly natural. But we are suspicious of a combination of part-time school and part-time home education, which might, at least initially, be administratively inconvenient (yet again) for teachers, but which might prove to have many compensatory advantages for all parties: flexi-schooling as a match to flexi-working, as Roland Meighan (1997) has suggested.

Whether a project is internal or external, it would be important to give a central place to student voice, that is, to treating the students as co-creators of the new approach. It is one of the characteristics of schools that there is a fear among adults of listening to students' views on either the shortcomings of current organisation and provision or the possibilities of alternative ways of doing things. Behind this fear is a recognition of student dissatisfaction, even among many of the best-behaved and hardest-working of students, but student voice can be rationalised away on the grounds that they are too immature to know what is good for them. The voice of the disengaged and disaffected is more easily discounted and invalidated. The evidence, however, suggests that the vast majority of students have highly cogent criticisms and constructive suggestions if they know their views are being taken seriously. (The minority who do not take the opportunity to speak seriously is easily detected.) But it would not just be a case of listening: this is important and is supported very strongly by the experience of business that much effective innovation has its origins in listening carefully to the views and wishes of customers and users. In education, however, the students would have to be active in the construction and evaluation of innovative alternatives, since if they do not share in the responsibility for what happens, they can readily fall back on blaming the teachers if new ways do not work out as hoped or planned. Getting agreement on what is to be learnt and how, in relation to what agreed outcomes – which will inevitably be much broader than those currently sanctified by government – is not achieved quickly or easily, but it is from such consensus that high levels of student motivation and effort stem.

Both internal and external projects for radical innovation share some basic problems with incremental innovation, namely, how we discover whether the innovations are any good, and in particular, any better than current practice, and if tried and properly tested, can then be disseminated widely round a system of over 24,000 schools, each of which values its limited, and therefore carefully protected, autonomy. Everyone in the education service talks about the importance of spreading good practice, but the record of so doing is very poor. Why?

The term itself is ambiguous and flabby. Often 'good practice' and 'best practice' are treated as synonyms, although clearly 'best practice' suggests a practice that has been compared with others and has proved itself better than other 'good' practices. Yet very rarely has there been any serious attempt to validate the innovation so that it can genuinely be said to be a good or best practice. Demonstrating this is not easy, of course, and for several reasons. Many innovations form just one new element of what goes on in the school or classroom and what is new is just one variable that interacts with other variables, making it difficult to trace cause–effect relations. The more radical the innovation, the more likely there will be what are known as Hawthorne-type effects. The sheer novelty of the innovation may be greeted as a welcome change from the routine and so the motivation and commitment of the participants tends to rise, but is not necessarily sustained when the novelty wears off; or again, the fact that the innovation is being researched and evaluated can itself change the behaviour of the participants with a positive effect of how they work. But it is essential to find ways of overcoming these problems if we are to be sure that innovations are indeed worth spreading more widely through the system.

Moreover much innovation in education is so varied in content and so thinly spread that it becomes difficult to collate evidence about its effectiveness. Schools like to choose their own topics and themes for innovation: there is no system by which 24,000 schools can agree that a limited number of topics or themes constitute priorities for innovation. It is this undisciplined 'let a thousand flowers bloom' approach to innovation that encourages governments to step in to control and direct innovation. But then there is a danger that the innovation, even though tested by committed volunteer schools, is seen by the rest of the system as an imposition, yet another 'initiative' rather than as something that has been co-created by practitioners and could be spread to every school.

It is one of the weaknesses of the government's current approach to innovation that the best ideas always have to appear to come from ministers, to be part of their political image and reputation. They feel that they can demonstrate their worth by innovation that is top-down. In reality, it rarely is. Many of the best ideas that flow from the DfES originated at school level, but they are spotted and taken up at the centre for what in the current jargon is called 'national roll-out'. The dissemination of innovation would work far better if, rather than being sucked out of a few schools into the DfES and then spewed back into the system as – you have guessed – another 'initiative', this vertical system of innovation or knowledge transfer were replaced by a *lateral* system that promoted direct exchange between schools and teachers through their own networks and communities of practice. David Miliband is the education minister who boasts at teacher conferences that he is unusual, even unique, in not being the author of a single initiative and he invariably gets a round of applause. Perhaps we are entering a new phase in which ministers do not think the specific ideas have to come from them, so spend less time in seeking new ideas and more time in providing the infrastructure by which the approach to innovation can be both more radical and more disciplined, and the outcomes can be more effectively tested and disseminated. In the public mind, when the system improves it is the ministers themselves who will get the credit, on the age-old basis of *post hoc, propter hoc*. Ministers do not need to be the source of innovation in schools any more than health ministers do for the practices of doctors in hospitals: getting the infrastructure right for transformation of public services through innovation is enough to do the trick.

That, of course, entails putting much more trust in the teachers as the key to engaging in the reforms that will establish the right foundations for lifelong learning. Do ministers have good grounds for placing such trust in the profession?

NINE

The teaching profession

People attracted to teaching tend to favour the status quo.... One cannot undo centuries of tradition with a few simple alterations. (Dan Lortie)

Without competent and motivated teachers, aspirations for a high quality education service are likely to founder. (OECD report on teachers)

In England trust is becoming scarce. Since Robert Putnam published his study of the decline of social capital in the US in 2000, there has been considerable interest in national variations in levels of trust. In Europe, Scandinavia is well ahead of other countries: around two thirds of the population agree that, generally speaking, other people can be trusted. In England and France this figure falls to under a third, even below the finding for the US.

In November 2001 Estelle Morris made a speech, issued as a pamphlet, entitled *Professionalism and trust: The future of teachers and teaching* (2001), in which she said "signals a new era of trust in our professionals on the part of Government". She specified as follows:

Teachers want the time and support to do what they do best – teaching pupils. That is why our proposals focus not just on the teacher's role but on the complementary roles that can and should be played by others in schools – like bursars, teaching assistants, technicians and learning mentors. In effect, we need to see a remodelling of not just the teaching profession but of schools, school staffing, school management and the use of ICT.

Eminently sensible, many of her audience might have thought, and their judgement would probably have been confirmed had they already been familiar with a mid-1990s study of secondary school teachers at work, which revealed that teachers spent only about one third of their time actually teaching, most of the remaining time being almost equally divided between administration and preparation. Surely Estelle Morris is right, her audience would judge, that most teachers would like to spend more of their time teaching and will therefore welcome the reforms.

In fact her proposals had a very mixed reception and were followed by a long period of opposition to workforce remodelling from one of the teachers' unions. Trust between politicians and teachers was at a very low ebb: the highly directive, top-down approach of the government between 1997 and 2001 had dismayed many teachers, and there was much talk of the 'deprofessionalisation' and 'casualisation' of teachers. The trouble with trust is that once it has been lost, the process of recovery is long and slow. Estelle Morris could not restore trust simply by *announcing* its return. Trust has to be demonstrated and earned, and many teachers remained suspicious and sceptical, for they felt that it might simply be a clever move by devious ministers to solve the problems of teacher recruitment and retention and the need to save money (since the half-baked and unpopular scheme for performance-related pay was proving to be unexpectedly expensive) by replacing teachers with assistants of various kinds, 'unqualified' people who, given responsibilities in classrooms in the absence of a real teacher, could only damage the quality of education. Suspicions of a 'hidden agenda' appeared to be confirmed by the leaking of a DfES paper in December 2003 which did not merely talk of reduced numbers of teachers but pointed out that legally a school needs to have no more than the head teacher as a qualified teacher!

Medicine and education are now public services that have grown dramatically over the last century, but they have taken very different routes in their professional structures. Doctors have for a long time been complemented by nurses, who have increasingly upgraded their qualifications and professional standing. Moreover, the boundary between what doctors and nurses are allowed to do is becoming more permeable, as nurses assume greater responsibilities. Moreover there are over 50 professional and para-medical specialties around the physicians and surgeons in hospitals and health centres. The standing of the qualified doctor has, as a result of this occupationally differentiated expansion, risen rather than fallen in terms of pay and prestige.

Teachers are not alone in spending too little time with the main client. Richard Horton, editor of *The Lancet*, is concerned at the lack of time doctors spend with their patients. A recent study has revealed that junior hospital doctors at night waste up to a third of their time answering bleepers unnecessarily, hunting down records and missing x-rays, and pushing patients on trolleys. Moreover, doctors can spend many hours writing routine prescriptions for painkillers or sleeping tablets for reasonably healthy patients. I suspect one of the reasons that many people opt for private medicine is that the doctors are willing to spend time talking with them. If teachers spend only about a third of their time actually teaching, and most of this in a busy classroom, just how much time can each *individual* pupil possibly spend in conversation with the teachers each day? And of the little time that is so spent, how much will actually be about the student's learning? Surely something is going wrong here? *Personalisation* and *personalised learning* must mean that more students should spend more time in individual interactions with teachers, teaching assistants, learning support assistants and other adults. *Personalisation* cannot be achieved, however, without workforce reform.

In his research Matthew Horne (2001) found widespread support among teachers for additional support staff, but unlike hospital doctors they have until recently worked largely as the lone adult in their classrooms, so it is perhaps not surprising that they also:

... viewed the prospect of managing other adults in the classroom as potentially challenging and rewarding. Teacher assistants increase the appeal of teaching as a career by reducing the level of individual workload and by increasing the level of teamwork in the classroom. However, teachers were adamant that they should not lose ultimate responsibility for pupils' learning and behaviour. A close working relationship between teacher and assistant should not disguise the need for a clear separation of professional responsibilities.

The government has specified 25 tasks, including chasing absentees, photocopying, record keeping and filing, that can be delegated to the assistant, and they are preparing a further tier in the hierarchy with the notion of the Higher Level Teaching Assistant, to match the Advanced Skills Teacher. But in reality it is very unlikely that there can ever be a clear separation of professional responsibilities, when it seems likely that around the teachers of the future there will emerge a larger and wider range of para-professionals as has happened in medicine. For why should assistants be just general-purpose aides to teachers rather than people who specialise in some distinctive aspect of education? Teachers, especially graduates in particular subjects, will often specialise in those subjects, without necessarily having this as their only specialism: assistants could specialise in some of the multiple facets of learning, rather than curriculum content, since much of their activity will be working with individual learners. There will always be some formal separation of roles between teachers and assistants, but a degree of role overlap is inherent for professionals who have to deal with people. What matters is teamwork in the service of the client. Just as a sensible newly qualified doctor can learn much from the experienced nurse, so the newly qualified teacher can learn much from the experienced assistant. There is now one teaching assistant for every four teachers; and if we include all kinds of support staff in schools, their numbers almost match those of teachers. As doctors are a minority but high status group in hospitals, teachers could in due course become a high status minority in schools.

This might be the path to a very different conception of the professional teacher. Between a third and a half of teachers leave the profession within five years, and the majority probably do not return. In learning to be a good teacher, one acquires many social and managerial skills that can be transferred to other occupations, and many 'mainstream' employers are beginning to recognise this. Motives for leaving the profession early are varied: some simply lose interest and look for a new challenge; some become exhausted; some think teaching is a job for a younger person. Lifelong careers are generally declining and there is no reason why teaching should not be included in this general trend.

Attention has naturally focused on this as a problem: the need for incentives to secure the retention of teachers, including 'golden handcuffs' (as though handcuffs made of any substance are the right way to ensure that teachers, like pupils, go willingly to school). The other side of this coin is that the profession is leaking into the community a regular flow of people, and of future parents, who know far more than average about the nature of learning and how it can be supported. This is potentially a huge resource, since it is known that children improve their learning when parents offer their active support. At the same time, it is worth remembering that the first inclination of many home-schoolers when faced with providing education at home is to attempt to behave like a teacher and turn part of the home into a schoolroom. Almost always they discover that this is a mistake, and that it is better to adapt the home into spaces for learning than to create a specialised learning space in it, and to fit learning into more natural rhythms rather than imposing a conventional timetable of subject studies. Ex-teachers may have lessons to learn if they become home-schoolers.

While what might be termed 'part-career' teachers already exist, less attention has been paid to the potential of a more usual form of part-time teacher. There are, of course, those who do not want full-time work, mainly married women, but there are also those whose work life is divided between teaching and some other occupation. The combination is difficult, since such people are often assumed by colleagues to lack full commitment to either job and can lose status and opportunities for promotion in both. In other cases, the time spent in school is seen as a temporary affair, done in the interest of public service to education, as with artists in residence. Yet such people often have huge credibility with students since their experience of the outside world is brought into school in a very vivid way and its relevance demonstrated. For many young people, the experience of co-learning with an adult is a refreshing change from being taught by a teacher: the difference is real.

As long as developments of this kind remain small-scale and at the margins, they do not need to threaten full-time, career teachers. Yet there is an argument for a significant increase in their numbers and for this good reason: they blur the boundary between teachers and ordinary adults and they also blur the boundary between learning in school and learning in life. Because so often these not-full-time-teachers are able to demonstrate that they are still active learners as well as teachers, they are visible models of lifelong learning. Their potential impact is huge, for students are more readily influenced by what teachers *do* than by what they say.

The presence of AoTs in school need not be a threat to the profession: in my experience AoTs are highly reluctant to claim any kind of expertise in teaching and are duly deferential to the profession. School is in many ways an artificial institution: the content of learning, the way learning is evaluated and the distinctive role of the teacher are unlike what happens in much of ordinary life and the learning that occurs there. We should not be surprised, therefore, to discover that teaching in the school requires a very special expertise, one commanding respect. But this should not lead us to neglect the existence and importance of other kinds of learning and teaching, even though the words 'learning' or 'teaching' may not be considered appropriate descriptions of such ubiquitous activities.

Students and staff themselves benefit when teachers see themselves as *brokers* of relationships between students and adults, both in schools and out, and as *boundary-spanners* across the divide between school and the wider world. In its origins, the school introduced a sharp break between the world as experienced by the rural child and its new destiny in the urban factory. Today it is through blurring both institutional and professional boundaries that the school can find its very different purpose in a post-industrial world. It is the best way in which to re-naturalise learning and thus establish sound foundations for lifelong learning. In the last 150 years of the life of the modern school, its responsibilities have grown massively. Today, I believe, we ask it to do too much and the strain on teachers – and students – shows. These educational functions of our society are achieved only when every adult is both a learner and a teacher in some form and every young person of school age knows it without being told. Most young people at the point of leaving school would be flummoxed by the questions 'What does lifelong learning mean to you?' 'In what way has your schooling prepared you for lifelong learning?'. Surely we should in due course expect a student to answer these questions as readily as ones directed to exploring the student's grasp of curriculum content or to articulating aspirations for higher education or the workplace.

All this is to be a longer-term development. In the short to medium term, most students will spend most of their formal education at, or under the control of, the school, and most of their time will be spent with qualified teachers. It is therefore important that they too be models of lifelong learning. This happens when teachers take action to make the school a learning organisation for themselves as well as for students, and when the profession defines itself as a community of learning. Fortunately, there is now a widespread conviction that this is a critical direction for the improvement of teaching and that the continuing professional development (CPD) of teachers must no longer be restricted to occasional, out-of-school courses for the individual practitioner, but must be set in the context of the school as a whole and a concurrent development of both organisation and staff in which teacher development is fused with their everyday practices. Thus it is that teamwork among teachers, mutual observation and support, action research projects based in classroom life, and similar activities blend CPD and the school as a learning organisation. Learning opportunities and plans and records are all needed for high quality teachers, but they need to be recognised by students, not shrouded in professional mystique, if they are to influence the attitudes and motivation of their fellow learners. CPD is not merely a sound investment in teacher and school improvement: it is a critical way in which teachers constantly demonstrate to their students that everyone is learning all the time and that this can be both profitable and pleasurable.

What kinds of leadership are needed to make schools learning communities and to lay foundations for lifelong learning?

TEN

Leadership

More leaders have been made by accident, circumstance, sheer grit or will than have been made by all the leadership courses put together. (Warren Bennis)

One of the hallmarks of effective leadership in this century will be the capacity to learn and adapt quickly. Years of experience will no longer be enough – and, in some cases, may prove a hindrance.... A winning characteristic of the new generation of leaders will be its commitment to personal learning and the ability to generate a 'buzz' about learning throughout their organizations. (Jay A. Conger)

The literature on leaders and leadership is enormous: the Google search engine offers some ten million references for each of these concepts. I suspect most of this, both generally as well as specifically in education, has been written in the last decade or so. Although there has been a stream of sociological and social psychological studies of leadership, the sudden expansion was in polemical tracts for business and industry, which later spread to public services such as education and health. It is the increasing importance, in the spheres of both policy and practice in education, of how leadership relates to school improvement and school effectiveness, that has dominated what has been thought and written. Indeed, the creation of the National College of School Leadership (NCSL) in 2000 is probably a reflection of, as well as a contributor to, this trend. NCSL may, at the same time, be an agent for promoting leadership for a deeper transformation that looks well beyond current structures, cultures and priorities in education

Does the concept of lifelong learning change the way we currently think about leadership in education? Does it provide a particular perspective on leaders and leadership? Probably. A commitment to lifelong learning as it affects school-age education focuses on particular educational outcomes, namely the preservation of the motivation to learn and the enhancement of the capacity to learn. But whether such educational purposes require a particular form of leadership has not been a topic of importance. Rather, the conception of leadership for school improvement and effectiveness has been heavily constrained by current policy and research outcomes, which emphasise the test performance and public examination results of young learners: it focuses on what students achieve in the present, not what they are to be and to achieve through their future learning. Leadership for student learning capacity may well not be the same as leadership for knowledge acquisition by students. For school leaders to give greater weight to the attitudinal and dispositional outcomes of education means that they must to some degree swim against the current drift of policy and be prepared to take a wider view of the aims of education and the school's vision, and use this to influence the priorities of teachers as well as the aspirations of students and the ambitions of their parents.

More importantly, the narrow conception of school effectiveness as performance on cognitive tests and examinations has led to a belief that outstanding educational leaders are those who can rescue or 'turn round' an institution that has been designated, in terms of test performances of students or judgements of OfSTED inspectors, 'a failing (that is, ineffective) school'. This conception is of a so-called 'charismatic' head teacher, a remarkably ill-defined term but one that, in the eyes of policy makers and their representations of such heads, is portrayed as a 'strong' or 'heroic' form of leadership. This tendency is amplified in media representations of head teachers, usually male, the most outstanding of whom become educational equivalents of John Harvey Jones, Richard Branson or Lord Browne. While such heads are firm of purpose and clear about priorities, with the strength of character to overcome resistance to change, they have a much wider and richer conception of education than appears in their popular representation. They enjoy a challenge and respond gloriously to crisis. "Les moments de crise", said Chateaubriand, "produisent un redoublement de vie chez les homes" – in Paul Auster's splendid translation: "human beings don't begin to live fully until their backs are against the wall". Yet they often reject the charismatic or heroic label and see themselves as enablers who, while not easily distracted from their vision, inspire and empower their colleagues to co-create the kind of school they believe to be within their collective grasp.

While ministers and senior officials ostensibly espouse the rhetoric of lifelong learning, national policies embody shorter-term and more concrete educational outcomes, and the best leaders are those who can ensure these outcomes, especially in circumstances where high test performances have not hitherto been achieved. It is constantly argued that priorities should focus on decreasing the numbers who have achieved no or few qualifications in the GCSE, or reducing the drop-out rates among 16- and 17-year-olds, or preparing more young people for life in the workplace; but it is only partially conceded that this might entail scrutinising and then reforming what happens in late primary and early secondary schooling, the periods when a significant minority become disaffected and disengaged and deep damage is done to their self-conceptions as learners. Schooling for lifelong learning, as noted earlier, seeks as outcomes of schooling that all young people should:

• view themselves as someone able to learn successfully;
• understand learning and themselves as a learner;
• leave school with a positive attitude to continued learning.

In the present climate, where there is such an emphasis on mastery of prescribed content that is easily measured in tests, there should perhaps be a fourth outcome: what Frank Coffield has called 'critical intelligence' or the ability to detect and challenge bullshit. Such different, or additional, purposes and outcomes of schooling probably require different leadership. Whether one starts positively from the dispositional ideals of lifelong learning, or negatively from what needs to be done to re-engage alienated adolescents, it is clear that leaders for lifelong learning must go beyond the dominant ethos and its narrow goals for schooling and be ready to challenge some of the fundamental assumptions we make about schools. To this end, leadership for lifelong learning can draw on two current themes in educational thinking: first, the distinction between management and leadership; and second, the conception of both schools and the teaching profession as learning communities.

Of course schools are complex organisations that have to be managed as well as led, but it is management issues that tend to predominate. This reflects several factors, such as the emphasis on the accountability of schools, both to governors and LEAs as well as central government, on school-based control over budgets, on parental choice and reporting to parents on student achievement, on teacher appraisal and performance-related pay, on school performance in league tables and OfSTED reports. Much of what was in the past managed outside the school is now an internal matter and the head takes responsibility for this with the ubiquitously termed 'senior management team' or, in the language of many a staff room, quite simply 'the management'.

As schools have grown in such internal complexity, management responsibility has been increasingly delegated to deputy heads, assistant heads, and senior teachers and heads of departments and teams of many kinds. My own experience of becoming 'an assistant master' at a grammar school with a head and just one senior master, but no deputy, seems far more remote from today than its mere 40 years. In that period, if most of us had any conception of our professional selves as managers, it was as managers of our classrooms, not the school. But for young teachers with an eye on promotion, this was the end of an era, as well as most of the grammar schools, and the beginning of the age of management. Management courses, with their emphasis on the skills of administration, and its associated competencies, and their banner of 'head teacher as chief executive', proliferated and prospered from the 1960s to the end of the 1980s.

At this point, the most influential figures in the mainstream literature of business, such as Peter Drucker and Warren Bennis, had moved firmly from management to leadership. Bennis, for example, offered this contrasting list in 1989:

- The manager administers; the leader innovates.
- The manager is a copy; the leader is an original.
- The manager maintains; the leader develops.

- The manager focuses on systems and structure; the leader focuses on people and culture.
- The manager relies on control; the leader inspires trust.
- The manager has a short-term view; the leader has a long-term perspective.
- The manager asks how and when; the leader asks what and why.
- The manager has his eye always on the bottom line; the leader has his eye on the horizon.
- The manager imitates; the leader originates.
- The manager accepts the status quo; the leader challenges it.
- The manager is the classic good soldier; the leader is his own person.
- The manager does things right; the leader does the right thing.

I can think of no brief overview that so succinctly captures and anticipates the major themes of the leadership literature in the following decade, when indeed so many books were written about leadership in education. Nor, I suspect, has there been much significant advance on them.

Despite current talk among policy makers of 'transformation' rather than mere 'improvement' in schools, and despite the current parallel in the literature of the concept of transformative leaders and leadership, the pressures, both real and perceived, on heads and senior teachers remain firmly on the left of the above list, stressing their roles as managers, namely people who administer systems, maintaining them through tight control over the immediately achievable, thus being 'the good soldier' who 'does things right', and who, in other words, delivers the government's agenda through a school that may be reduced to being a delivery unit.

And to a degree there is nothing wrong with that, for schools are indeed organisations that have to be managed. The point is that management is not enough. For Bennis, the essential difference between leaders and managers is that between those who master the context and those who surrender to it. Because the context of government education policy is often so narrow and short term, those whom it calls the leaders of schools are likely to tie themselves to that agenda and thus be better managers than leaders. The irony is that many of the heads who in the event do deliver the agenda most brilliantly are actually looking far beyond the immediate context and it is their very capacity to do so that makes them so successful: they manage for delivery of the government agenda but lead beyond it. Paradoxically heads who are compliant to this agenda and who seek to manage it often find themselves doing so effectively enough, but are not able to achieve the level of excellence to which the policy makers aspire, for that demands leadership too. When policy makers raise the stakes – usually in the form of higher targets – the demand can seem unreasonable and puts pressure on the head as manager. It is the head with an eye on the horizon that finds it easier to cope with a changing bottom line.

Over the years I have shared the Bennis list at many a conference of school senior staff, many of whom took the view that an effective school needs both managers and leaders as defined. Over time, I have become less and less satisfied with this formulation, for two reasons. First, if deputy heads are the managers in the Bennis list, this is hardly a good preparation for headship if a head is the leader on the Bennis list. Second, I have come to think that if we really need the kind of leadership that Bennis describes, then we also need a different approach to management, one grounded in a view of the school in which both leadership and management responsibilities are shared or distributed and in which the two are designed to be compatible and coherent, rather than merely complementary and contrastive. This means that we derive good management practice from new conceptions of leadership, whereas the pressures have been to infer the features of good leadership from what in recent years have been new conceptions of management. Transforming leadership may depend on transforming management too. The meaning of 'transformation' to policy makers may be little more than an increasing rate of improvement to meet yet more challenging targets, but 'transformational' leadership is something very different. Leithwood, Begley and Cousins (1994) consider:

> ... the central purpose of transformational leadership to be the enhancement of individual and collective problem-solving capacities of organizational members; such capacities are exercised in the identification of goals to be achieved and the practices to be used in their achievement.

An essential feature of sound leadership is the ability to increase the capacity of members of the school community to overcome obstacles to implementing their vision more successfully and with greater ease – which is just another way of saying that they too must *learn how to learn* and apply new learning effectively in the interests of the community. Thomas Sergiovanni (1992) speculated that the types of leadership being encouraged might paradoxically be inhibiting the process of school improvement. The real key to school improvement, he suggested, might be transforming schools from organisations into communities, thus opening up what has proved to be a most productive line of analysis and argument over the last decade by a wide range of writers on education. In schools that are learning organisations:

- learning is a continuous, strategically used process, integrated with, and running parallel to, work;
- learning takes place in individuals, teams and with the other organisations and communities with which the school interacts;
- learning is the outcome of the collaboration that springs from a commitment to self-monitoring, self-evaluation and self-improvement.

Do we really have to devise and foster quite new models of leadership if we want to transform schools for lifelong learning? We are in the realms of what Jim Collins calls 'Level Five leaders' (2001). He is not concerned with the lower levels of leadership (One to Three) but with the crucial difference between good (or Level Four) leaders and those who make the leap to become great ones (Level Five) in the world of business and industry. There are many good leaders, but few great ones. The most vibrant economy will be that which can move more leaders from Level Four to Level Five, from good to great. It is arguable that in education, too, there are many good leaders, but few great ones, and that the future of the system depends on getting more heads to move from good to great, not just on getting the weak heads to become good ones.

The argument, then, is not that great heads will be those who take lifelong education most seriously or espouse it most explicitly or preach it most persuasively. Rather, it will be those who look to transcend the immediate context, responding to its demands but with a richer vision that provides the *conditions* under which the fundamentals of lifelong learning – learner motivation and an enhanced capacity for learning – are most likely to be realised. Such leaders may embrace the kinds of reform suggested in Chapter Seven, not because they will help to realise lifelong learning for all, but because they are a way of providing better education for school-age children.

These features are evident in educational leaders in much (not all) of what Collins finds to be the characteristics of Level Five leaders in business. His basic finding is very close to the outstanding heads described in the opening paragraphs. Level Five leaders are modest, reserved, understated yet wilful and fearless. They do not want to be larger than life heroes, do not long to be put on a pedestal, do not have a gargantuan ego, and do not become dazzling charismatic figures. These Level Five leaders:

- have high ambitions for their organisation, not themselves;
- talk about their organisation, not about themselves;
- maintain a dogged, unwavering, ferocious resolve;
- are fanatically driven with an incurable need to produce sustained results;
- apportion credit to events outside themselves when things go well;
- take personal responsibility when things go badly;
- can be likened to plough horses rather than show horses;
- set up their successors for even greater success.

Strikingly, they do not have a vision to which they seek to convert their staff. Rather they surround themselves with the right kind of staff and then work with them to create a shared vision. Most school governors want to be persuaded by every applicant for a vacant headship that he or she has a wonderful vision, one that contrasts with what has gone before, and after appointment can produce a roadmap of where to drive the bus – that is, they want a Level Four head. By contrast, the Level Five head is more concerned to get the right people on the bus and then figure out with them where to drive it. Replacing staff is more difficult in education than in business. I find it significant that most heads who have been brought into a failing school to 'turn it round' appear to be extremely skilful in managing to engineer the early departure of many of the existing staff, vacating seats on the bus for the essential replacements.

Level Five heads evince a ruthless honesty with themselves, and face the facts, however brutal they might be. They harbour no false hopes and peddle no wild dreams. But with this reality check, they have an unwavering faith that success will eventually come. They keep the core message simple and constantly reiterate it with great passion. They are, in Isaiah Berlin's famous terms, hedgehogs who know one great and wonderful thing rather than wily foxes who know many things and see great complexity in everything. (This might explain why successful academics, who are foxes, rarely make a Level Five head or policy maker, and vice versa.) Everything is bent to this central, simple vision. Thus ICLT, in particular, is pursued not as a fad or fashion or from wanting to be first on a bandwagon, but because it fits with what is needed and can accelerate, but not create, momentum towards it.

Transcending the immediate context *for lifelong learning* entails some distinctive additions to Level Five, and most of these relate to a richer conception of learning. Level Five leaders believe that the organisation's vision must be shared, not by conversion to that of the leader, but through a process of co-creation. Leaders for lifelong learning extend this to a conviction that all teachers can and must learn and can and must contribute to the task of leadership. They are cautious, even sceptical, about hierarchy because this allocates authority on a sliding scale of status levels and thus inhibits the distribution of leadership opportunities as they arise in relation to who in what context has something particular to offer.

The other side of distributed leadership is distributed learning. One acquires the authority to lead when one has learned and is ready to learn again. Leaders for lifelong learning thus demand of themselves that they should be model learners: the head teacher becomes the head learner. This is essential if students are to come, through the school years and associated education in various forms, to a firm conviction that one can and does learn without being taught in a classroom, and that this is merely one form of learning with its own strengths and weaknesses. Teachers are fellow learners both in school and outside it, and if students do not understand this, then their education has made them, at best, excessively dependent on formal education. Part of the difficulty is that there is no ready discourse with which to challenge the conventional roles of teacher and student and to forge the new conceptions and relationships that embody new approaches to institutional learning.

Leadership for lifelong learning thus involves a commitment to *communities of learning,* of which the school is one, or perhaps more accurately, a confluence of many. For around every school there are natural communities built on age, sex, ethnicity, class and religion, as well as natural communities that cut across these categories, and all potentially flow into the school, and then in new, multi-category streams on the way out. We are in part *talking our way into* these communities of learning; in part we shall have to begin to live inside them in order to find the language to describe and explain what they are.

Schools contain pre-existing communities, what are nowadays called 'communities of practice', which Etienne Wenger defines as:

... groups of people who share a concern, a set of problems, or a passion about a topic, and who deepen their knowledge and expertise in the area by interacting on an ongoing basis.... [They] are a natural part of organisational life. They will develop on their own and many will flourish whether or not the organisation recognises them. Their health depends primarily on their members and on the emergence of internal leadership.

The community aspect refers to members who interact, learn together, build relationships, and develop an identity and sense of belonging based on mutual commitment. The practice aspect denotes a set of socially defined ways of doing things: common standards and agreed routines that create a basis for action, communication, problem solving, performance and accountability. It is clear that the staff of a school often form a community of practice – professional educators – one that subdivides into smaller and often tighter communities of practice around the subjects of the curriculum or pastoral functions. All these communities are constrained by their histories and by the structure of what counts as the school in its ubiquitous and recognisable form: as such they will tend to resist change. So many teachers, after years of experience of a school day divided into neat blocks of lesson, acquire a default mode of action that is normal within the community of practice and constantly reinforced by the hierarchical structure of power and authority. Yet, as Wenger notes:

You cannot cultivate communities of practice in the same way you develop traditional organisational structures. Design and development are more about eliciting and fostering participation than planning, directing and organising their activities.... What managers have been missing so far is an understanding of the kind of social structure that can take responsibility for fostering learning, developing competencies and managing knowledge.

So leadership for lifelong learning means reworking the very nature of the community we call the school: the school as a learning community is not simply a school that puts greater emphasis than in the past on the importance of learning. In an institution in which learning is for and by every member of the community, its structure and culture will be different, reflecting new kinds of relationship among teachers, between teachers and students, and among students, especially *mentoring*, with enquiry and problem solving as institutional norms.

Such communities will readily evolve into networks – networks within the school between different communities of practice, networks with other schools or formal educational institutions, and networks with the wide range of communities of practice that we generally call the wider community beyond the school. The NCSL rightly distinguishes six levels of learning for its Networked Learning Communities (NLCs).

Pupil learning: NLCs are expected to have a clear pedagogic focus at the heart of their activity. In particular, the programme focuses on the development, application and evaluation of a wide range of evidence-based approaches to raising levels of pupil achievement across the networks.

Adult learning: the NLC programme is about creating school cultures in which teachers learn with and alongside their students. It emphasises the value and effectiveness of practitioner enquiry and collaborative approaches to staff learning, including but not restricted to coaching, mentoring, study groups, enquiry partnerships, work shadowing, classroom observation and school visits.

Leadership for learning and leadership development: the NLC programme seeks to invest in the capacity of head teachers, network leaders and other leaders within schools to create the enabling conditions for network learning. Creating a culture that encourages professionals to change their practices and organisations to experiment and take risks requires strategic leadership. Establishing and sustaining knowledge-creating and knowledge-sharing networks will not happen without new kinds of leadership beyond that offered by conventional head teachers and middle managers. The programme assumes a much wider pool of latent leadership talent than the system currently harnesses.

School-wide learning: the NLC programme is designed to support the development of schools as professional learning communities. It aims to transform schools into learning organisations, capable not just of doing what they currently do better, or responding more effectively to current demands and environment, but of generating a capacity for continuous innovation, adaptation and recreation. In this respect, the programme differs markedly from other 'initiatives' that focus only on particular school management issues, teaching practices or curriculum areas. Schools have assumed the role of recipients of change, responding to new central demands and having accountability defined through standardised frameworks from without. This programme seeks to restore the capacity of schools and leaders to change themselves.

School-to-school learning: the most distinctive feature of the NLC programme is the idea that teaching professionals will generate and share more knowledge through working together than in isolation. This rationale is based on a number of assumptions, the most important of which is that the best way to encourage teachers to share knowledge within a school is also to get them to share knowledge with others outside the school.

Network-to-network learning: a key premise of the NLC programme is that while networks help the schools within them to develop local solutions to the problems they face, schools in other networks should also be able to understand and interpret these solutions and transpose them into their own contexts.

This approach to school leadership is likely to foster the kind of change explored in this book as gateways to lifelong learning, although this would demand, as schools look outward, they do so not merely to other schools in their network but to the rich, untapped educative resources in the wider community.

I do not know how many of the Level Five heads known to me would see themselves as missionaries for lifelong learning. But I am convinced of three things. First, they are wholly committed to the fundamentals of lifelong learning, including the motivation to learn and the capacity to do so. Second, they have the qualities and skills to shape a school and its members and stakeholders in a way that makes it likely that those fundamentals will be achieved, not as an alternative to conventional success, but as a wondrous addition to it. Third, they have an insight into the strengths and the weaknesses of the education system as they find it, so they are the constructive critics who are most likely to point to the policy changes that will lead most surely to the leadership of communities of learners and thus to a society of lifelong learning.

But can school leaders alone establish the right foundations for lifelong learning at school level? Or does that require a new leadership from politicians and ministers?

ELEVEN

Firm foundations

Education itself is often the most powerful predictor of high levels of social capital. Educated people and educated communities have skills and resources that enable them to form and exploit social networks more readily, whereas less educated communities have to struggle harder to do so. But investment in education as a condition of social-capital building rarely appears in our stories. (Putnam and Feldstein)

Personalisation, by definition, means direct involvement in the production process by what we still call the consumer. Such co-creation poses a significant challenge to many of the fundamental distinctions of the industrial era, especially that between supply and demand. (Riel Miller)

The government's education policy for schools has in recent years been painted in terms of the demands of a knowledge-based economy and the need for greater social cohesion, but in practice has been determined by what is often called 'the standards agenda', a commitment to improving the quality of schools, teachers and teaching in order to raise levels of student achievement. None of these policies was directly shaped by concerns about lifelong learning; but neither was any policy intended to damage lifelong learning. It is the contention of this book, however, that this has in fact been the effect of some of those policies. If we are to develop policies that intentionally and explicitly support lifelong learning, on what existing policies must they build? Can the changes be made in ways that nevertheless maintain a degree of continuity and coherence with past policies?

The worst crime a politician can commit is to make a U-turn: the media and opposition parties are unsparing whenever they spot or suspect such a lapse. So when ministers make changes or adjustments to their policies – a perfectly natural and reasonable activity for the rest of us in our personal, professional and public lives – they have to pretend that they are doing no such thing. It would be easy to conclude this book with a list of new policies that would create a radically different education service in a different, but unspecified, society. Doing so would avoid the irritating complication of having to specify what being 'there' would look like and what needs to be done to get from here to there. It makes more sense to explain how we arrived here in the first place, for there are always some continuities as well as discontinuities in evolution, and then to explore the potential for adjusting policies, on the basis of the five themes that have served as threads through our discussion of the school years, to make policy more compatible with an explicit commitment to a society in which lifelong learning flourishes.

The hand of history always helps to shape how the present might unfold into the future, as it did when the Labour Party introduced its education policies for schools back in 1997. To the surprise of many of their supporters on the Left of the Party, there was an acceptance of the principles of 'diversity and choice', since *Choice and diversity: A new framework for schools* had been the title of a 1992 White Paper by the Conservatives. It dealt with five major themes: quality, diversity, parental choice, greater school autonomy and greater accountability. In the preface, the then Prime Minister John Major set out the principles on which the proposals rested:

> ... more parental choice; rigorous testing and external inspection of standards in schools; transfer of responsibility to individual schools and their governors; and, above all, an insistence that every pupil everywhere has the same opportunities through a common grounding in key subjects.

Labour education policy maintained considerable continuity here. Although the grant-maintained schools were abolished, grammar schools survived and specialist schools were expanded; the testing regime and the inspectorate under Chris Woodhead were strengthened; and the literacy and numeracy strategies were designed to support the basics.

Diversity ensures choice and choice drives up standards: this was the thesis. As the Conservatives' White Paper put it:

> Greater diversity has offered parents and children greater choice.... More diversity allows schools to respond more effectively to the needs of the local and national community.... Uniformity in educational provision presupposes that children are all basically the same and that local communities have essentially the same educational needs. The reality is that children have different needs. The provision of education should be geared more to local circumstances and individual needs: hence our commitment to diversity in education.

For some in the Labour Party, that in government their own ministers should pursue this policy with enthusiasm, and indeed more assiduously and more imaginatively than the Conservatives, was a betrayal of the principles behind the comprehensive school, which officially was to be 'modernised' rather than abandoned. (Today we can also see the hint in this quotation of what has become *personalisation*.) Labour was also to face the tension between the autonomy and accountability of schools, seeing autonomy and reduced accountability as a reward for conformity to much greater central direction which exceeded even that of the Conservatives after their conversion to the National Curriculum and national testing.

This was a government impatient to raise standards: thus the insistence on targets throughout the system, from ministers down to individual pupils. The result of Labour's commitment to diversity and choice, when combined with published measures of school performance through OfSTED reports and league tables of student assessments to inform parental choice, greatly increased competition between schools to attract and retain students. As with the Conservatives, these policies were to be the drivers of educational excellence: indeed, *Excellence in schools* was the title of Labour's 1997 White Paper. This could be described as a plan for *system excellence*, for it was the top-down imposition of policies, initiatives and interventions that were intended to improve the quality of teaching and learning in every school.

A critical difference between Conservative and Labour philosophies, however, was that whereas Conservatives were committed to *equality of opportunity*, New Labour replaced both this and the older socialist belief in *equality of outcome* with the notion of *excellence for everyone* or *universal excellence*. In the words of the 1997 White Paper:

> The demands of the future will require that everyone succeeds in secondary education. We are not going back to the days of the 11-plus.... We intend to modernise comprehensive education to create inclusive schooling which provides a broad, flexible and motivating education that recognises the different talents of all children and delivers excellence for everyone.

In Labour's second term it was recognised that this could not be achieved by the policies of the first term, or at least not by them alone. There had been hints during the first term that to achieve excellence for everyone, or *personal excellence* as well as *system excellence*, would require less central control and much more local innovation, and the commitment to innovation became more explicit during the second term – as noted in Chapter Eight. The 'individualised support' for pupils and the provision of mentors in 2001 were to evolve into the ideas of *personalisation* in 2003, by which it was understood that networks of schools and teachers could contribute to local innovation as well as disseminating the outcomes of innovation. Suddenly, it seems, ministers were rediscovering the value of collaboration between schools, a quality that is essential to the lateral strategies that were developing alongside vertical (or top-down) ones.

So policies have evolved, but remain in tension, as shown in Figure 2. Competition and collaboration are not necessarily wholly antithetical, but can coexist in a creative tension, as has been demonstrated in the business world. It is not a matter of choosing between the two, but of making them work productively together with as many benefits and as few unintended side-effects as possible. But this does not apply to trust. The policies that drove system excellence created an education service characterised by low trust between ministers/DfES officials and schools and their staffs – despite much rhetoric to the contrary. Policies now emerging to drive personal excellence require a service with high trust among the participants. Low trust works only for short periods in extreme circumstances when high trust will not work. A return to high trust has now become essential, and without it the undoubted gains made during the period of low trust are potentially at risk (see Figure 2).

This would, however, require a different conception of the education service and thus a different approach from ministers and the DfES to how they lead it. Indeed, it is arguable that they have been so busy *managing* the system they reformed that they have failed to offer the *leadership* by which there could and should be a different kind of service from the one they inherited in 1997. There has been continuity in policy and there have been advantages to this. But there has also been significant evolution. The questions are: evolution into what? and how fast? and will what emerges be more consonant with a philosophy of lifelong learning? For a positive answer to these questions, we must look at schools in a new way.

Policy makers, like academic experts in school effectiveness, hold to a model of the operation of the school in terms of *input–process–output*: the *input* consists of resources, material and human; the *process* includes leadership, school organisation and teaching; and the *output*, especially for ministers, is best summarised by student performance in tests and examinations. This model, which forms a key element of the continuity between Conservative and Labour education policy assumptions, does not fare well in reflecting the issues raised

Figure 2: The development of New Labour policy

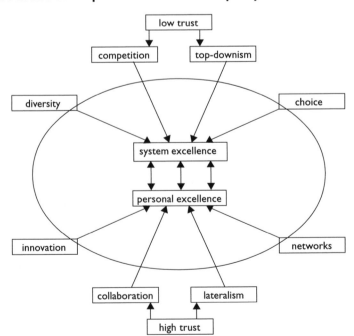

in this book – or, of course, what happens in most schools in the name of education. A different model is needed to describe and explain what happens in schools, and to demonstrate how education at this point is where the foundations of lifelong learning can be firmly laid. The central concepts involved are just four types of *capital* – material, intellectual, social and organisational.

The most familiar form of capital is *material capital*. This includes financial capital as well as physical capital such as buildings and equipment, which could in principle be realised as money. All organisations have to manage their material capital; schools are rarely rich in material capital, and although attractive premises and lavish equipment are desirable, material assets do not in themselves make for a good school.

People are a more important resource to a school. *Intellectual capital* embraces what we usually call human capital, or the education and training of individuals, with allied concepts to cover a broader spectrum – their knowledge, skills, capabilities, competences, talents, expertise, practices and routines. Intellectual capital is one of the invisible assets of an organisation and complements its material assets. Schools are evidently rich in the intellectual capital of the teachers and staff, but also of the students, their families and communities. A successful school mobilises the complete range of its intellectual capital by employing outstanding teachers and support staff and using their talents to the full; by realising all the abilities of the students and endowing them with a wide range of knowledge and skill; and by drawing on the intellectual capital of parents and other adults who can potentially serve and contribute to the school.

Another of a school's invisible assets is its *social capital*, which is also about people, and in particular the character and quality of their relationships. Social capital has both cultural and structural aspects. Culturally, social capital consists in the *trust* that exists among head, staff and students and also between the school's members and its various stakeholders; structurally, social capital is the extent and quality of the *networks* among its members – between head and staff, staff and students, staff and parents – as well as the school's networks with external partners. A school that is rich in social capital has a strong sense of itself as a community, with ties to other communities.

These three forms of capital have different effects when they are used. Material capital is often reduced when it is used – you cannot spend money and keep it – although accumulated wealth can also be devoted to the production of other goods. Intellectual capital, by contrast, does not deteriorate when it is given away – sharing my knowledge with you does not deprive me of the knowledge. Social capital actually increases as it is used – if I trust you, you are more likely to reciprocate my trust, and our mutual trust grows.

The fourth type of capital, *organisational capital*, refers to the knowledge and skill among the members of an organisation about how to deploy the intellectual and social capital to maximal advantage. A most important element of organisational capital is the recognition by leaders that high levels of social capital – trust – is essential to exploiting to the full the available intellectual capital. Great school leaders have organisational capital in abundance. They know not only how to deploy the school's existing intellectual and social capital, for instance in ensuring that teaching is of the highest quality, in creating positive relationships so that everyone feels both challenged to give their best but are supported in doing so, and in drawing into the school the intellectual and social capital of its various stakeholders and partners. Such leaders also know how to *increase* the school's intellectual and social capital. In part this is a matter of deploying material capital as an investment in developments that explicitly enhance the school's intellectual and social capital. In part it means choosing policies and practices that are capital-rich in preference to those that are not; and this clearly rests on the ability to recognise that most policies and practices have implications, sometimes hidden, for intellectual and social capital. In recent years we have begun to realise that in many organisations, including schools, the intellectual and social capital are under-estimated and under-used. This is because the managers and leaders lack the insights and skills that comprise organisational capital, or because, as with schools, they are under external pressure to drive the organisation in a way that distracts them from the task of deploying their intellectual and social capital to best advantage and distorts the outcomes.

This mobilisation of capital, and the knowledge of how to increase it, is quite simply a measure of the organisation's *capacity*, especially the capacity to manage change and improvement, processes that demand, and are fuelled by, high levels of social and intellectual capital. The capacity to manage change is especially important when an organisation is under severe pressure to change and improve its performance. This is currently the case, where ministers have changed the vocabulary from school *improvement* to *transformation*. The irony is that while ministers have demanded deep change in a short timeframe, their policies have unintentionally weakened the system's social capital when it was critically needed to provide the capacity for such change. Without substantial investment in the education system's social capital, the potential intellectual capital cannot be realised in full, and transformation will be impossible.

In any organisation, high levels of internal capital, into which available external capital has also been harnessed, yield high capacity. But to do what exactly? Not merely to do the job at hand, but to do things differently in order to do them better. In other words, one expression of high capacity is readiness to innovate. The mobilisation of intellectual capital fosters new ideas and creates new knowledge that leads to successful innovation in making the school more effective. Such innovation creates new professional practices so that teachers work smarter, not harder. Innovation requires high levels of intellectual capital, which is a necessary but not sufficient condition. Innovation also requires high levels of social capital, the trust between head and staff and among staff to engage in the new practices and risk taking that are inherent in innovation. Moreover the social capital also generates the internal networks by which new professional practices can be transferred from one teacher and classroom to another; and the external networks may well be the source or spark of an innovation. In the most effective schools, the best professional practices – which are of course a form of intellectual capital – are not locked inside the heads of a few outstanding teachers and learning assistants and restricted to the privacy of their classrooms, but through the knowledge sharing arising from high levels of social capital, become the common property of all who might profit from them.

The pathway to better and more innovative schools is through simultaneous investment in the four forms of capital. There is no other route. As the chapters in this book have sought to show, the four capitals work together in complex ways that are positive but not amenable to detailed control from the centre. If schools merely implement innovations that are devised elsewhere and then mandated or imposed upon them, they may, to a degree and for a period, become better schools, but they will not be innovative schools and their underlying capacity for innovation and for sustaining change may be weakened rather than strengthened.

Schools that are capital-rich will endow their students as well as their staff with strong intellectual and social capital. These are the very qualities constantly advocated by those describing the prerequisites of a better society: intellectual capital to meet the needs of a knowledge-based economy and social capital for high levels of social cohesion and political participation. A better society demands that the outcomes of schooling and the processes of education be broadened to embrace the very qualities that characterise a particular conception of society and the good life within it.

But the demands of lifelong learning mean that we must look more closely at the relationship between what happens in school not only to society in general, but also to the rest of the education service in which so much lifelong learning is embedded. The four forms of capital capture the 'growth potential' not merely for an individual school but also for schools collectively. As schools strengthen their external networks, all the participants in the networks potentially enhance their levels of intellectual and social capital. Since inter-school networks have to be positively led by committed heads, the sharing among them potentially increases their own organisational capital too. This is why federations and collegiates, as discussed in Chapter Seven, are potentially important: they require high levels of capital to develop, but once underway they generate yet more capital. An education service that consists of autonomous, isolated schools cannot generate additional, shareable capital. In consequence, there cannot be the innovation networks on which the rapid transformation of the system depends; nor will there be the impetus and means to turn the education system as a whole, including central government, into a learning system.

Using the terms 'intellectual', 'social' and 'organisational' capital also provides us with a way of reading across from schools to other organisations, to communities and to society as a whole, so that we see how the same underlying forces that characterise good schools are also the crucial features of good partner organisations and good local communities and the good society. Internal and external capital are interdependent and often mutually reinforcing. A school may draw on the intellectual and social capital of its partners and stakeholders, but it also contributes to theirs in return as a virtuous circle. Capital-rich schools are an essential basis of a capital-rich society, for it is intellectual capital that enables the knowledge-based economy, social capital that enables social cohesion, and organisational capital that enables policy makers and practitioners at all levels to mobilise the intellectual and social capital to the common good. Such a society enshrines, and has the capacity to practise, lifelong learning.

Where is the DfES in all this? As it has shifted the focus of the content of its reforms, as indicated in Figure 2, it has also changed its *mode of intervention*. In principle, there are two ways that policy makers intervene in their government of the education service. The *directive mode of intervention* is characterised by a heavy programme of legislation and regulation in order to control the system. To ensure compliance with the regulation and prescription, strong measures of inspection are introduced along with increased mechanisms for accountability. As much funding as possible is earmarked so that schools allocate their resources as centrally intended and not according to local preference, which is unlikely to be consonant with central stipulation. There is no school in England that is unfamiliar with this mode of intervention, for it has dominated education policy for some years.

There is another way, the *enabling mode of intervention*. Here legislation is minimal and regulation is reduced. Funding for schools is determined by what can be afforded and as much as possible is left to local decision on the grounds that local knowledge is essential to the allocation of resources according to need, importance and urgency. The task of the centre is mainly concerned with articulating broad directions for the service, providing a conducive climate, monitoring progress and offering feedback, and most of all helping to broker the many partnerships on which the effective operation of the education service depends. In short, the DfES has a responsibility to work to increase the system's intellectual and social capital by modelling high trust and providing the essential architecture and support for flourishing networks. It needs to move from telling the system what to do to developing its own form of organisational capital, one that enhances the intellectual and social capital of the very system it serves.

Many people in the education service prefer the enabling to the directive mode. But of course it is not really a matter of choice, but of balance. And while there are signs of movement towards a more enabling mode, more movement is needed towards the enabling mode from ministers and officials to get the balance right. The greatest challenge is the transformation of the *education system*, not just schools, into a learning system that is rich in all four forms of capital. For the DfES to become a learning organisation and more effective in reaching its goals, it will, like the best schools, have to learn how to draw on the high levels of intellectual, social and organisational capital in so many of its 25,000 partner schools. And this will not happen unless the DfES rethinks and re-engineers its relationship to the rest of the education service.

This deep shift is essential if lifelong learning is ever to become a reality in terms of its foundations in schools and school-age education. For the five themes that run through the argument of this book – learning how to learn, generic skills, the project, mentors and personalisation – all have roots in some aspects of DfES policy and are already growing fast in some schools and classrooms. Without more active nurturing from the centre, they will not flourish – and neither will lifelong learning.

Change at central government in relation both to its mode of intervention and to the five themes will, of course, entail changes in particular policy areas, especially where current policies are destructive of the foundations of lifelong learning. The most promising area is *personalisation*. The concept is currently under development. Neither ministers nor their officials are entirely sure what it means – and that state of affairs is to be welcomed, since it means we can all share in determining what it means in principle and practice. Personalised learning will develop quite quickly in 14-19 education and training where much of the focus is on tailoring curricula, courses and pathways to meet a wide variety of student needs and aspirations. It will develop much more slowly and with more difficulty in key stage three where personalisation will be less about curriculum choice but more about pedagogy, and changing the structure of the school day and year, to meet student needs. It is here that the *project* has particular potential, for the national curriculum can be loosened and adapted in ways that maximise student engagement. Without innovative personalisation in key stage three, there will continue to be student disengagement and underperformance in key stage four and poor participation rates in post-16 education and training.

Robert Putnam (2000) has recently shown how a wide variety of projects can contribute to restoring social capital in American society – and some of these projects are explicitly educational, involving young people. These projects take time and energy to create and then embed in the life of the community. Where young people are involved in such projects, they – like their teachers – experience distributed leadership. It should be no surprise that the people who are most actively engaged in the community in middle age are precisely those who had experience of projects during their adolescent years.

If bold experiments and pilots into a transformed key stage three are brokered from the centre, then *learning how to learn* and *generic skills* will soon find their natural place, for it is in key stage three that some of the most exciting work is already taking place. This should be able to build on what happens in key stage two if the positive elements in the government's primary school strategy, as outlined in *Excellence and enjoyment*, are allowed to flourish.

But *learning how to learn* and *generic skills* offer their greatest challenge to what has dominated so much education policy, namely formal assessment as an internal driver of what happens in school and as the main mechanism for the accountability of schools through league tables. At present no minister objects if *learning how to learn* and *generic skills* are successfully acquired by pupils – indeed policy makers would applaud the achievement – but only as long as they do not interfere with national tests and public examinations. In fact, the evidence from research on assessment for learning is that learning how to learn actually *enhances*, rather than detracts from, test performance. It will be essential to provide more evidence that it is not a matter of having to choose between alternatives, and that doing both is vital. We then have to find ways in which we can record student achievement in *learning how to learn* and the *generic skills*, not only as a way of informing students and their parents, as well as employers and higher education, but also as a way of broadening what we consider to be the outcomes of schooling, for which schools are ready and willing to be accountable.

Enriching the nation's intellectual and social capital are drivers of much government policy because they are keys to the good life. They are rightly drivers of education policy too. Using these concepts to understand what now happens in schools and during the school years opens up new possibilities of what could and should happen. Preparing people for lifelong learning can no longer be an implicit goal of school education: it has now to be an explicit driver of policy for schools. Firm foundations for lifelong learning can be laid in the school years. The argument is undeniable; the action in policy and practice is in part already underway; we need only the imagination and will to reach the proper conclusion.

Sources and suggestions

Foreword
DfEE (Department for Education and Employment) (1998) *The learning age: A renaissance for a new Britain*, London: The Stationery Office.

Chapter Two: Curriculum
Barber, M. (1996) *The learning game*, London: Gollancz.
Bayliss, V. (1999) *Opening minds: Education for the 21st century*, London: RSA.
Gardner, H. (1999a) *Intelligence reframed*, New York, NY: Basic Books.
Gardner, H. (1999b) *The disciplined mind*, London: Simon & Schuster.
Stenhouse, L. (1975) *An introduction to curriculum research and development*, London: Heinemann.
Warnock, M. (1977) *Schools of thought*, London: Faber & Faber.

Chapter Three: Assessment
Black, P., Harrison, C., Lee, C., Marshall, B. and Wiliam, D. (2003) *Assessment for learning: Putting it into practice*, Buckingham: Open University Press.
Clarke, S. (2001) *Unlocking formative assessment*, London: Hodder & Stoughton.
James, M. (1998) *Using assessment for school improvement*, London: Heinemann.
Skidmore, P. (2003) *Beyond measure: Why educational assessment is failing the test*, London: Demos.

Chapter Four: Pedagogy
Bayliss, V. (1999) *Opening minds: Education for the 21st century*, London: RSA.
Bayliss, V. (2003) *Opening minds: Taking stock*, London: RSA.
Bentley, T. (1998) *Learning beyond the classroom*, London: Routledge.
Claxton, G. (1997) *Hare brain, tortoise mind*, London: Fourth Estate.
Claxton, G. (2000) *Wise-up: The challenge of lifelong learning*, London: Bloomsbury.
Gopnik, A., Meltzoff, A.N. and Kuhl, P.K. (1999) *The scientist in the crib: Minds, brains and how children learn*, New York, NY: Morrow & Co; published in the UK as *How babies think: The science of childhood*, London: Phoenix.
Holt, J. (1964) *How children fail*, Harmondsworth: Penguin.
Jackson, P.W. (1968) *Life in classrooms*, New York, NY: Holt, Rinehart & Winston.
Joyce, B., Calhoun, E. and Hopkins, D. (1997) *Models of learning – Tools for teaching*, Buckingham: Open University Press.
Lave, J. and Wenger, E. (1991) *Situated learning*, Cambridge: Cambridge University Press.
Rose, J. (2001) *The intellectual life of the British working class*, Harvard, NY: Yale University Press.
Rudduck, J. and Flutter, J. (2004) *How to improve your school*, London: Continuum.
Seltzer, K. and Bentley, T. (1999) *The creative age*, London: Demos.
Steinberg, A. (1998) *Real learning, real work*, London: Routledge.

Chapter Five: Advice and guidance

Bayliss, V. (1999) *Opening minds: Education for the 21st century*, London: RSA.

Bayliss, V. (2003) *Opening minds: Taking stock*, London: RSA.

Bridges, W. (1995) *Jobshift*, London: Nicholas Brealey.

DfES (Department for Education and Skills) (2003) *21st century skills*, London: DfES.

DfES (2003) *Towards a unified e-learning strategy*, London: DfES.

Gardner, H. (1993) 'Opening minds', *Quarterly*, issue 1, pp1-5, London: Demos.

Handy, C. (1989) *The age of unreason*, London: Business Books.

Illich, I. (1971) *Deschooling society*, London: Calder & Boyars.

Reich, R. (1991) *The work of nations*, New York, NY: Alfred Knopf.

Social Exclusion Unit (1999) *Bridging the gap*, London.

Chapter Six: Information, communication and learning technologies

Crowther, D., Cummings, C., Dyson, A. and Millward, A. (2003) *Schools and area regeneration*, Bristol: The Policy Press.

Cuban, L. (2002) *Oversold and underused: Computers in the classroom*, Yale, NY: Harvard University Press.

DfES (Department for Education and Skills) (2003) *Towards a unified e-learning strategy*, London: DfES.

Illich, I. (1971) *Deschooling society*, London: Calder & Boyars.

November, A. (2001) *Empowering students with technology*, London: Pearson.

Oppenheimer, T. (2003) *The flickering mind: The false promise of technology in the classroom*, London: Random House.

Stationery Office, The (2003) *Every child matters*, London.

Steiner, G. (2001) *Grammars of creation*, London: Faber & Faber.

Steiner, G. (2003) *Lessons of the masters*, Yale, NY: Harvard University Press.

Chapter Seven: School design

Annesley, B., Horne, M. and Cottam, H. (2002) *Learning buildings*, London: Demos.

Bayliss, V. (1999) *Opening minds: Education for the 21st century*, London: RSA.

Crowther, D., Cummings, C., Dyson, A. and Millward, A. (2003) *Schools and area regeneration*, Bristol: The Policy Press.

Chapter Eight: Innovation

DfEE (Department for Education and Employment) (1997) *Excellence in schools*, London: DfES.

DfES (Department for Education and Skills) (2001) *Schools: Achieving success*, London: DfES.

DfES (2003) *Excellence enjoyment*, London: DfES.

DTI (Department of Trade and Industry)/DfEE (2001) *Opportunity for all: In a world of change*, London: DTI.

Fielding, M. and Bragg, S. (2003) *Students as researchers*, Cambridge: Pearson.

Greany, T. and Rodd, J. (2003) *Creating a learning to learn school*, Stafford: Campaign for Learning.

Hargreaves, D.H. (2003) *Education epidemic: Transforming schools through innovation networks*, London: Demos.

Hesselbein, F., Goldsmith, M. and Somerville, I. (eds) (2002) *Leading for innovation*, San Francisco, CA: Jossey-Bass.

MacBeath, J. (2003) *Consulting pupils: A toolkit for teachers*, Cambridge: Pearson.

Meighan, R. (1997) *The next learning system: And why home-schoolers are trailblazers*, Nottingham: Educational Heretics Press.

Thomas, A. (1998) *Educating children at home*, London: Cassell.

Chapter Nine: The teaching profession

BECTA (British Educational, Communications and Technology Agency) (2003) *Family learning: A guide to practice*, Coventry: BECTA.

Campbell, R.J. and Neil, S.R. (1994) *Secondary teachers at work*, London: Routledge.

Horne, M. (2001) *Classroom assistance*, London: Demos.

Lucas, B. and Smith, A. (2002) *Help your child to succeed*, Network Educational Press.

Morris, E. (2001) *Professionalism and trust: The future of teachers and teaching*, London: Social Market Foundation.

Putnam, R. (2000) *Bowling alone*, London: Simon & Schuster.

Chapter Ten: Leadership

Bennis, W. (1989) *On becoming a leader*, London: Hutchinson.

Collins, J. (2001) *Good to great*, London: Random House.

Leithwood, K., Begley, P.T. and Cousins, J.B. (1994) *Developing expert leadership for future schools*, London: Falmer Press.

Sergiovanni, T.J. (1992) *Moral leadership*, San Fransisco, CA: Jossey-Bass.

Wenger, E. (1998) *Communities of practice*, Cambridge: Cambridge University Press.

Chapter Eleven: Firm foundations

Adey, P. and Shayer, M. (1994) *Really raising standards*, London: Routledge.

DfES (Department for Education and Skills) (2003) *Excellence and enjoyment*, London: DfES.

Fukuyama, F. (1995) *Trust*, London: Hamish Hamilton.

Putnam, R.D. (2000) *Bowling alone*, London: Simon & Schuster.

Putnam, R.D. and Feldstein, L.M. (2003) *Better together*, London: Simon & Schuster.

Participants in the seminars

Curriculum
Jo Armitage, Qualifications and Curriculum Authority; Valerie Bayliss, RSA; Tom Bentley, Demos; Pete Dudley, London Borough of Redbridge; Mary James, University of Cambridge; Michael Wilkins, Outwood Grange School, Wakefield.

Assessment
Patricia Broadfoot, University of Bristol; John Dunford, SHA; David Hanson, IAPS; David Hawker, Brighton and Hove LEA; Ron McLone, OCR; Dylan Wiliam, King's College, University of London.

Pedagogy
Guy Claxton, University of Bristol; Charles Desforges, University of Exeter; Iain Hall, Parrs Wood High School, Manchester; Caroline Hobbs, Sir Charles Lucas Arts College, Colchester; Bill Lucas, Campaign for Learning.

Advice and guidance
Cathy Bereznicki, Guidance Council; Gary Forrest, Qualifications and Curriculum Authority; Chris Humphries, City and Guilds; Pat Morgan-Webb, New College, Nottingham; Sue Taylor, Learning and Skills Development Agency; Tony Watts, OECD.

ICLT
Jonathan Clarke, Scottish Enterprise Glasgow; Lorna Cocking, Pearson plc; Clare Johnson, Key Stage Three Strategy; Owen Lynch, BECTA; Chris Yapp, Hewlett Packard.

School design
Parin Bahl, Capita; Hilary Cottam, Design Council; Matthew Horne, Demos; Martin Tollhurst, London Borough of Newham.

Innovation
Lindsey Bagley, Ufl; Christopher Ball, educationist; Donald Clark, Epic Group plc; Anne Diack, Innovation Unit, DfES; Mike Gibbons, Innovation Unit, DfES; Patrick Hazlewood, St John's School and Community College, Marlborough, Wiltshire.

The teaching profession
Carol Adams, GTC; John Bangs, NUT; Frank Coffield, University of Newcastle upon Tyne; John Dunford, SHA; Tamsyn Imison, educationist.

Leadership
Jean Gledhill, John Kitto Community College, Plymouth; David Jackson, National College for School Leadership; John McBeath, University of Cambridge; Nigel Middleton, Head Support Ltd; Tim Moralee, Thomas Estley Community College; Anita Wright, Woodmansterne Primary School, Lambeth.

Governance
Patrick Diamond, Cabinet Office; Derek Grover, NHSU; Ian Johnston, Glasgow Caledonian University.

Plenary session
In addition to the above: John Craig, Demos; Mark Cummings, DfES; Bob Fryer, NHSU; Nicholas Stuart, consultant; Ken Wardop, Scottish Enterprise Glasgow.

Index

Numbers in *italics* refer to figures

A

absenteeism 60, 77
accountability 68
action research 79
adaptability 81
adolescents 59, 62, 83
adult education centres 56
'adults other than teachers' (AoTs) 59, 62, 76, 78
AfL, *see* assessment for learning
age cohorts 58, 59
alienation, *see* disaffection
AoTs, *see* adults other than teachers
apprenticeships 13, 29-30, 61
architecture 55
Arnold, Matthew 6
assessment
  amount of 15
  core subjects 22
  categoric 18
  cost of 19, 22
  effect on curriculum 16
  ICLTs and 48
  motivational aspects 24
  need for reform 15
  ownership of 19
  purpose of 20-1
  quality of 16
  standards 15-16
  stress of 15
  summative 23
  teachers and 19, 20
assessment for learning (AfL) 23, 24, 32, 48-9
assessment specialists 42
assistant head teachers 83
Association for Science Education 12
attitude 6, 28, 39, 82
authority 34

B

babies 26
BBC 53
BECTA, *see* British Educational and Communication Technology Agency

behaviour vi, 59, 64

Bennis, Warren 83, 84, 85
'big ideas' 12
Black, Paul 29, 32, 33
blaming 68, 72
Blunkett, David iv
boredom 9, 10, 13
'bricks' 10, 11
Bridges, William 35, 36
British Educational and Communication Technology Agency (BECTA) 47, 53
Brown, Ann 31-2
budgets 83
Building Schools for the Future 55
buildings, constraints of 32, 55-64
bursars 75

C

Campaign for Learning 70
capacity 10, 27, 81-2, 96
capital 95, 96, 97, 98, 100
careers 35, 36-41
casualisation, *see* deprofessionalisation
charisma 82
chartered examiners 22, 23
choice
  diversity and 92
  extension of 62
  in curriculum 63
  Labour acceptance of 92, 93
  limited by schools 63
  parental 6, 57, 58, 83, 92
  in comprehensive schools 8
  reversibility of 6
citizenship 11, 70
citizenship education 6, 39
classroom design 56
Claxton, Guy 29
coaching 42
Coffield, Frank, 83
college of further education 61
colleges, guidance in 38
collegiates 58, 61, 97
Collins, Jim 85, 86
communication 12, 17, 51, 61

communities 57, 58, 87, 95, 97
  of inquiry 32
  of learning 52, 87-8, 89
  of practice 32, 87-8
community centres 56
community education 56
competences 11
competition 93
comprehensive schools 8
computers, *see* information,
  communication and learning
  technology
Confederation of British Industry (CBI)
  41
confidence, with ICLT 46-8, 53
Connexions 36, 37
continuing professional development
  (CPD) 79
continuity 9
core subjects 22
CPD, *see* continuing professional
  development
creativity 28, 32, 65
criterion referencing 19
critical intelligence 83
critical thinking 40
criticism 72, 90
Cuban, Larry 50
cultural transmission 6
culture 6, 29, 30, 42
  teenage 59
cumulative learning v
Curriculum Online 53
curriculum, *see also* National
  Curriculum
  'basic' content 45
  competence-led 11
  'dumbing down' of 7, 11
  choice in 63
  compulsory 8, 13
  debate about 5, 10
  definition 5
  determination of 5
  development 13
  functions of 5-7
  knowledge in 11
  language for 13, 14
  meaning of 14
  nature of 9-12
  of apprentices 29
  personalisation and 99
  provision 13
  skills in 11

customisation 62, 63, *see also*
  personalisation

D

decision making 37
Department for Education and Skills
  (DfES) 1, 15, 46, 52, 65
  as learning organisation 98
  changes in approach of 98
  policies 99
Department for Education and Skills,
  segmentation of 57
deprofessionalisation 75-6
deputy head teachers 83, 85
DfES, *see* Department for Education
  and Skills
directive mode of intervention 98
directories 42
disaffection 72, 82, 83
disapplication 8, 9
disengagement 36, 60, 61, 63, 72, 82
dispositions 6, 28, 82
diversity 92, 93
dropouts 9, 51, 82
Drucker, Peter 65, 83

E

educational research 25
'edutainment' 50
e-learning team 53
e-mail 46
employment 35-41, *see also* work
enabling mode of intervention 98
enterprise 12
entitlement 8-10, 18
entitlement curriculum 8
entrepreneurship 12
equality 93
e-teaching 53
Every child matters 57
evidence-based approaches 89
examination boards 15, 16
examinations
  distorting effects of 23
  emphasis on 81
  excessive use of 15
  generic skills and 99
  quality of 16
  as measure of school effectiveness 82
  use of results 21, 81
examiners 22
excellence 93

experience, areas of 10
extended school, *see* school, extended

F

facilities 58
failing 68
families 95
federations 58, 61, 97
feedback 21, 31, 98
  computer-generated 49
fields 10
filing 77
'five I's' 29
flexi-schooling 71
flexi-working 71
formative assessment 23
funding 98

G

games 48
Gardner, Howard 10, 12, 42
generic skills, *see* skills, generic
golden handcuffs 77
good practice 72
governors
  accountability to 83
  radicalism and 70
  preferences for 'level four' head
    teachers 86
  transfer of responsibility to 92
grades 18, 22, 23
graduate-as-learner 40
grammar schools 8, 83, 92
grant-maintained schools 92
Guidance Accreditation Board 41
Guidance Council 41

H

half-way houses 61
Handy, Charles 35, 36
Hawthorne effects 72-3
head teachers
  BECTA support for 47
  charismatic 82
  ICLT and 51
  investment in technician support 50
  leadership qualities 82-90
  network learning and 89
  relations with government 68
  relations with the community 58
  training 53

Health and Safety at Work Act 41
heritage 5, 6, 7, 8, 9, 10, 14
hierarchy 87
high culture 6
higher education v
Hirst, Paul 10
Holt, John 27, 31
home schooling 70-1, 78
Horne, Matthew 76
Horton, Richard 76
human capital 95

I

IAG, *see* information, advice and
  guidance
ICLT, *see* information, communication
  and learning technology
ICT Test Beds project 69
ICT, *see* information and
  communication technology
Illich, Ivan 41-2
imitation 29, 34
incentives, for teachers 20, 77-8
individualised support 93
industrial revolution, legacy in schools
  69
informal processes 42
information and communication
  technology (ICT) 45, 75, *see also*
  information, communication and
  learning technology
information, advice and guidance (IAG)
  36, 37, 38, 41, 42
information, communication and
  learning technology (ICLT) 45-54,
  69, 87, *see also* information and
  communication technology
infrastructure 52
initiatives 66, 71
innovation 65-74
  as expression of high 'capacity' 96
  definition of 65
  government support for 67
  incremental 66, 69, 72
  in schools 97
  lateral 73
  methodological 66
  organisational 66
  radical 66
  risk taking and 68
input-process-output model 94
inspectors 82
instrumental attitude 18

integrated humanities 11
intellectual capital 11, 95, 96, 97, 98,
  100
Internet 45, 46, 48, 49, 50, 53
invention 12

J
Jackson, Philip 28
job vacancies 41

K
key processes 12
key skills, *see* skills, key
key stage tests 18
key stories 12
knowledge
  acquisition 27, 82
  assessment of 17
  bodies of 11
  forms of 10
  importance of 6
  in National Curriculum 11
  in schools and apprenticeships 30
  lateral transfer of 52, 73
  learning and 27
  local 98
  sharing of 97
  skills and 11
  transmission 7
  work-related 61
knowledge economy 12, 25, 28, 34, 35,
  37, 66, 91, 97, 98
knowledge society 28

L
labour market 37, 41
language acquisition 26
languages, modern foreign 8, 9
lateral thinking 40
Lave, Jean 29
leadership
  as rescuing institutions 82
  characteristics of effective 81-90
  charismatic 82
  distinguished from management 83-4
  distributed 87, 99
  educational outcomes and 82
  for innovation 47
  for knowledge acquisition 82
  for learning 89
  for learning capacity 81-2

'level five' 85-7, 89-90
literature on 81, 84
policy and 81, 82, 84
political 90, 94
promotion of 81
school effectiveness/improvement and
  81, 84
transformational 85
use of organisational capital by 95-6
willingness to challenge of 82-4
league tables 19, 21, 68, 83, 93
Learndirect 53
learning
  capacity 26, 27, 51, 81
  definition 27
  distributed 87
  graduate 40
  informal 9-10, 70
  natural 31
  network-to-network 89
  NLCs and 88-9
  on-the-job 25, 61
  personalised 63, 76
  school-to-school 89
  school-wide 89
  situated 29
  student 40
  vocabulary 29
  work-related 39
Learning age, The iv
learning and skills councils 41
learning communities 52, 87-9
learning styles 63
learning support assistants 76
learning how to learn, *see also* meta-
  learning
  achievement in 100
  acquisition of 40
  'assessment for learning' and 23, 33
  as entitlement 18
  as generic skill 12
  as preparation for work 13
  description of 27-8
  enhancing learning capacity 27
  ICLT and 47, 48-9
  important for later learning 2
  leadership and 85
  policy and 99
  teaching 33
  vulnerability of 17-18
learning webs/networks 42
leaving age 6, 7, 22, 58-9, 60
lecturers 26
legislation 98

lessons 30, 33, 51
leverage 32
Lifelong Learning Foundation v
literacy 8, 45
literature 7, 8
local education authorities (LEAs) 41,
   53, 83
low achievers 24

M

Major, John 92
malpractice 19
managed learning environments (MLEs)
   52
management 83-5, 94
management courses 83
marking 22
marks 23
material capital 95, 96
Meighan, Ronald 71
memorisation 27
mentoring 13, 25, 42, 88
mentors
   'adults other than teachers' as 59, 60,
      62, 75,
   for on-the-job learning 25
   importance for lifelong learning 2
   learners as 31, 59
meta-cognition 28
meta-curriculum 28
meta-learning 27, 29, 32, 33, 37, *see also*
   learning to learn
Miliband, David 55, 73
ministers
   as source of ideas 73
   attitudes to change 19, 20, 66, 67, 91
   effect on social capital 96
   home education and 71
   innovation and 65, 68
   response to ICLT 45, 47, 51
mistakes 60
MLEs, *see* managed learning
   environments
mnemonics 28
mobile telephones 46, 48, 66
moderation 22
Morris, Estelle 75, 76
Morris, Henry 56
motivation
   agreement important for 72
   as goal of lifelong learning 70
   'assessment for learning' and 23, 24
   changing perceptions of vi, 7

effect of projects on 32
factors reducing 17-18, 21
heritage and 7, 8, 14
ICLTs and 47, 48
'level five' leaders and 90
preservation of 34, 81
school years as important for 1
teachers and 9, 10
tests and 21-4
multiple intelligences 10
music festivals 32

N

National College for School Leadership
   47, 81
National Curriculum 8, 9, 11, 92
   assessment of 17
   curriculum development and 13
   review of 39
   scepticism about 12
National Information Advice and
   Guidance Board 41
National Qualifications Framework 37
national roll-out 73
natural learning 14
neighbourhood learning centre 57
networked learning communities
   (NLCs) 88-9
networks 51, 88-9, 93, 95, 96, 97, 98
New Opportunities Fund (NOF) 46
norm referencing 19
numeracy 45

O

observation 29
occupational qualifications 38
OfSTED 68, 82, 83, 93
Opening Minds project 11, 63, 70
Open University 54, 69
organisational capital 95-8

P

para-professionals, *see* support staff
parents
   ambitions of 82
   as source of careers guidance 37
   beneficial effects on education 57
   choice 6, 57, 58, 83, 92
   effect of choice of school 57, 58
   home teaching and 70
   ICLT and 52

radicalism and 70
right to know children's achievement
   21
school attitudes towards 58
security expectations of 56
parent-teacher relationships 52
part-time schooling 71
pathfinder project 69
Patten, John 19
pay 19, 76, 83
pedagogical counsellor 42
pedagogy
   change in 47
   function of 27
   personalisation in 63
   versus 'natural' teaching 25
peer pressure 37
peer-matching communications
   network 42
performance
   of schools 19, 20, 21, 24, 82, 93
   of teachers 19, 20
   on tests 99
performance-related pay 76, 83
personal advisers 36-7
personal data assistants (PDAs) 46
personal excellence 93
personal, social and health education
   (PSHE) 6, 39
personalisation 2-3, 63-4, 76, 91, 92, 93,
   99
photocopying 77
planning 37, 71
plays 32
policies
   adjustments to 91
   DfES 99
   drivers of 100
   effect on trust 93
   for excellence 93-4
   leaders and 81, 82, 84
   learning to learn and 99
   New Labour *94*
   short-term nature of 82, 84
   top-down 93
policy makers 51, 52, 60, 84, 94, 98
political participation 97
portfolio working 35, 37
post-16 retention 38
preparation *5*, 6, 14
problem solving 12, 17, 28, 88
professional development 61
progression *5*, 9, 12, 14, 35

projects 2, 31, 32, 33, 34, 40, 51, 60-4,
   99
   external 70-71, 72
   importance of co-creation 72-3
   internal 69-70, 72
   student voice in 72
promotion 78
psychological boundaries 59
public opinion 60
Putnam, Robert 75, 99

Q

qualifications
   A-level 9, 15, 19, 22
   AS-levels 15
   CSE 18
   GCSE 15, 18, 19, 22-3, 46
   GNVQ 22-3
   occupational 38
   O-levels 18
   Qualifications and Curriculum
      Authority 21
questions 32-3

R

reading 8
record keeping 77
reference service 42
regulation 98
Reich, Robert 35, 36
relationships 31, 32, 88, 95
research 12, 28, 79
resource allocation 98
revolution 67, 68
Royal Society of Arts (RSA) 11, 70
RSA, *see* Royal Society of Arts

S

school education 1, 2
school halls 56
School Leadership for Information and
   Communication Technology
   (SLICT) 47
schools
   administration of 58
   alternative terms for 57
   as artificial institutions 78
   as communities 85
   as learning organisations 89
   capital-rich 97, 98
   comprehensive 92

contrasted with apprenticeship 30
design 55-64
extended 33-4
facilities 58
failing 82
growth potential of 97
ICLT-rich 51
organisation 51
organisation of day 34
performance 19, 20, 21, 24, 82, 93
post-industrial purpose 79
primary 58, 82
secondary 82
specialist 62, 71, 92
standards in 92
structure of day 32
transformation of 67, 84, 85, 96, 98
underuse of 55
withdrawal of children from 70
year-group structure 58-9, 63
schooling, outcomes of 100
Secondary Heads Association 22
self-esteem 18
Sergiovanni, Thomas 85
Shakespeare, William 7, 8
simulations 28
situated learning, *see* learning, situated
skill exchange 42
skills
  acquisition 7
  entrepreneurial 39
  evaluation 17, 28, 37, 49
  forecasts 41
  generic 2, 12, 17, 28, 31, 40, 49, 60,
    64, 99, 100
  in National Curriculum 11
  information, communication and
    learning technology 40, 46
  interpersonal 40
  key 11, 17
  knowledge and 11
  levels 41
  literacy 40
  numeracy 40
  reading 8
  research 49
  self-diagnosis 37
  self-management 37
  transferable 6
  work-related 61
SLICT, *see* School Leadership for
  Information and Communication
  Technology

small and medium-sized enterprises
  (SMEs) 61
social capital 91, 95-100
social cohesion 91, 97, 98
Social Exclusion Unit 36
social reproduction 6
socialisation 6
soft skills, *see* skills, generic
software 52
spell checks 49
standardisation 63
standards 15-16, 92, 93
standards agenda 91
status 77, 78, 87
Steiner, George 54
stress 15, 19
student-as-learner 40
student-curriculum broker 42
students
  as project co-creators 72
  aspirations of 82
  university 40
  suggestions 72
summative assessment, *see* assessment,
  summative
support staff 76, 77
Sutton Centre (Nottingham) 57
system excellence 93

T

targets 19, 20, 68, 84, 93
teacher training 62
teachers,
  analogy with doctors 76
  appraisal of 83
  as brokers 79
  as learners 34, 89
  assessment of 19, 20
  assumptions of 33
  consent 70
  contribution to leadership 87
  curriculum change and 13-14
  deprofessionalisation of 75-6
  discourse of 28-9
  incentives for 20, 77-8
  intellectual capital of 95
  learning from failure 68
  new technology and 46-50, 52
  non-teaching tasks 75
  part-career 78
  pay 19
  priorities 82
  'professional' 42

qualities needed by 40
questions of 32-3
role of 9, 10, 27, 49, 62, 75
senior 83, 84
skills of 11, 23, 77
training 53
views of assessment 19
teaching assistants 75, 76, 77
  higher level 77
teaching
  as art or science 25
  as telling 27
  home 70
  improvement of 25
  of 'learning how to learn' 33
  pedagogy versus natural 25
  using Internet 53
teamwork 12, 40, 61, 77, 79
technical support (technicians) 50, 75
technology 45-50
teenagers, *see* adolescents
testing 92
tests 18, 68, 81, 82, 94, 99
  computer marking of 22
  quality of 16
texting 46
thinking skills 28, 32
'three R's' 29
'three T's' 68
Tomlinson Working Group vi, 20, 38,
  40
top-down initiatives 52, 73, 75
Towards a skills revolution 41
training 41, 53, 95
transformation 67, 81, 84, 85, 96, 98
transition management 37
trust 73, 75, 84, 93-4, 95, 98
tutors 26

U

understanding
  assessment of 17
  in National Curriculum 11
unemployment 36, 61
university admission policies 16-17

V

values 6
village colleges 56
vision 86
vocational courses 40
vocational education 13

vocational options 37
vocational subjects 23, 37, 38
vocational/academic distinction 38
vocationalism 11
voluntary bodies 69
voluntary processes 42

W

Wagner, Etienne 29
Warnock, Mary 12
Watson, Thomas 68
Wenger, Etienne 87
Wiliam, Dean 29, 32, 33
Woodhead, Chris 27, 92
work 13, 25, 34, 61 *see also* employment
work-related learning 13
work-related learning, *see* learning,
  work-related

Also available from The Policy Press

A new deal for children?

Re-forming education and care in England, Scotland and Sweden

Bronwen Cohen, Peter Moss, Pat Petrie and Jennifer Wallace

Paperback £19.99 (US$29.95) ISBN 1 86134 528 3
234 x156mm 256 pages June 2004

Creating a learning society?

Learning careers and policies for lifelong learning

Stephen Gorad and Gareth Rees

Paperback £19.99 (US$32.50) ISBN 1 86134 286 1
Hardback £50.00 (US$75.00) ISBN 1 86134 393 0
234 x156mm 208 pages May 2002

The Learning Society and people with learning difficulties

Sheila Riddell, Stephen Baron and Alastair Wilson

Paperback £19.99 (US$32.50) ISBN 1 86134 223 3
234 x156mm 260 pages May 2001

Learn to succeed

The case for a skills revolution

Mike Campbell

Paperback £19.99 (US$29.95) ISBN 1 86134 269 1
Hardback £50.00 (US$79.95) ISBN 1 86134 392 2
234 x156mm 128 pages May 2002

Differing visions of a Learning Society

Research findings Volume 1

Edited by Frank Coffield

Paperback £21.99 (US$37.50) ISBN 1 86134 230 6
Hardback £50.00 (US$75.00) ISBN 1 86134 246 2
216 x148mm 288 pages July 2000

Differing visions of a Learning Society

Research findings Volume 2

Edited by Frank Coffield

Paperback £18.99 (US$29.95) ISBN 1 86134 247 0
Hardback £50.00 (US$75.00) ISBN 1 86134 248 9
216 x148mm 248 pages November 2000

The right to learn
Educational strategies for socially excluded youth in Europe
Edited by Ides Nicaise
Paperback £19.99 (US$34.50) ISBN 1 86134 288 8
234 x156mm 432 pages November 2000

Forthcoming

Balancing the skills equation
Key issues and challenges for policy and practice
Geoff Hayward and Susan James
Paperback £22.99 (US$38.95) ISBN 1 86134 575 5
Hardback £55.00 (US$79.95) ISBN 1 86134 576 3
234 x156mm 224 pages tbc October 2004

Social capital and lifelong learning
John Field
Paperback £35.00 (US$55.00) ISBN 1 86134 543 7
234 x156mm 176 pages tbc February 2005

To order further copies of this publication or any other Policy Press title please contact:

In the UK and Europe:
Marston Book Services, PO Box 269, Abingdon, Oxon, OX14 4YN, UK
Tel: +44 (0)1235 465500, Fax: +44 (0)1235 465556,
Email: direct.orders@marston.co.uk

In the USA and Canada:
ISBS, 920 NE 58th Street, Suite 300, Portland, OR 97213-3786, USA
Tel: +1 800 944 6190 (toll free), Fax: +1 503 280 8832,
Email: info@isbs.com

In Australia and New Zealand:
DA Information Services, 648 Whitehorse Road, Mitcham, Victoria 3132, Australia
Tel: +61 (3) 9210 7777, Fax: +61 (3) 9210 7788,
E-mail: service@dadirect.com.au

Further information about all of our titles can be also be found on our website:

www.policypress.org.uk